THE GOOD Brand

How Companies Create Valuable Brands

Michael Lasky, J.D.

www.brandcentering.com

Published by *Perimeter Communications*

ISBN 978-0-9975281-0-7

Printed in USA

The Good Brand

More information on the topic of this book can be found at:

www.BrandCentering.com

The author can be reached at:

mlasky@BrandCentering.com

Special Sales:

Bulk purchases are available by contacting sales@brandcentering.com

Second Printing 2016

Book cover design by Srdjan Plavsic

How Companies Create Valuable Brands

Table of Contents

Introduction

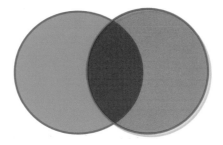

The Good Brand

There is a great deal of (unseen) money in your company. It's just sitting there for the taking.

The money is the value of your brand, and it should be your most valuable asset. If it is not, then your company's brand is not doing its job as well as it could be.

Valuable companies are those that have figured out how to capture their brand's value and convert it into real profit. In public companies, this means higher market valuations; for privately held companies, this means the company can fetch a substantially higher sale price when it is later sold.

So, how do you build a more valuable company?

The short answer: building a brand-centric company, i.e., a company whose brand assets are *huge*, takes skills from two disparate fields, legal and marketing.

For the most part, people in these two fields do not, or cannot, cross over the knowledge gap dividing them even though doing so can be very profitable when building a brand. The fact is, building and marketing a brand is not intuitive to most people, including people who consider themselves experts in business.

Of course, there are thousands of books about brand marketing. In researching this book, I read many of them. The most striking feature of these books is that very few recognize the two most fundamental rules of branding: 1) If no one can own the brand, you can't either, and 2) If you don't own your brand, you are never going to build a brand. These rules will be explained in Chapters 4 and 5 of this book.

Likewise, I have read most of the legal textbooks on trademarks, and they universally have nothing to say about brand positioning and how it fits with Rules 1 and 2.

It is no wonder, why successful brand building is practiced by so few companies. No one tells the *whole* story.

This book is intended to tell you the whole story, including the fundamentals you need to harvest the brand value of your company. In it, you will learn why so many businesses are merely profitable, while others are both very profitable and extraordinarily valuable. Everybody thinks they know how to build a brand, but as you will see, there are skills to learn and rules to follow.

The following example illustrates how elusive building a brand can be.

You know this image: Energizer Bunny. It is the core brand of a battery company. A brilliant creation. Unforgettable. So why did the company abandon their strongest image?

It is about the company's failure to understand how brand building works. Even though *advertising* and *brand building* have the same goal, to enhance the business' value, they are can be at odds with each other because advertising often has a very short outlook.

In the 1990s, the Energizer company produced 155 commercials featuring a pink bunny. It was a phenomenal success, yet, by the end of the decade, the company had gotten tired of the bunny and relegated him (her?) to a minor role in its advertising. What had started out as a gimmick to poke fun at Duracell, which had its own animated animal in Europe, had become **the essence of the brand identity.** The Energizer Bunny (EB) was not some *adjunct* to the brand, it *was* the brand itself. Its importance transcended the name *Energizer*. No doubt more people recognized the bunny image over the name Energizer, yet the bunny was put out to pasture.

It took 10 years for the company to rediscover EB, and now it's back. Even so, 10 years is a long time, and many young buyers have never seen the amazing commercials that made EB famous.

Because the company underestimated the value of EB as a brand, a lot of money was left on the table. A lot of brand equity was lost.

Why would a company do that?

Such questions, and many brand strategy questions, will be addressed in this book. The mere fact that such things are done with great brands, even by smart companies with vast resources, says that brand building is not intuitive.

Furthermore, just because a company has built *one* great brand does not mean it can repeat that success – unless it understands how a successful brand is created in the first place. In the case of the Energizer Bunny, one has to at least realize that a brand, even one born by accident, can't be *managed* by accident. There must be a strategy based on what has worked consistently.

In fact, most companies with successful brands often do not know how they achieved brand success, and those that *do* know often lose that knowledge during a management change or when the company changes marketers.

One of the most common brand killers is boredom. Brand managers get bored with the same image over the years. New marketers come along with the goal of "freshening up" the brand, but their real intention is to show that they are better/smarter than their predecessors. The result is often the loss or destruction of a valuable brand.

The missing link is this: brands are valuable because they consistently deliver the same message. Customers are not bored. They depend on the brand as a symbol of enduring connection, which is why they became customers in the first place. If you change your brand image – perhaps you have changed the contents of the product also – then the *brand promise* of consistency is broken.

Those of us who are not fortunate enough to have been born with *brand genes* have to learn the brand formula until it becomes second nature.

A Very Important Warning

In this book there will be lots of examples. A few of the examples will be companies you've never heard of. These lesser-known companies are hard to use as examples because you can't compare your own knowledge of their brand. So, most of the examples will involve companies you *do* know. Some of them are very large, but of course, they all started out very small. There is a natural tendency to view these examples as aberrations, or at least not applicable to your business. Try to resist that tendency because it will cause you to miss the message of the book, which is this: these branding principles are fundamental. They will work for all companies, regardless of size and nature of business.

Also be aware that you really *can* emulate these successful companies. Do not get distracted by the fame or size of the examples we use. Remember that in every one of these examples, the company was once much smaller than your company. What is important is to remember *how* they got where they are and how you can borrow from their success.

The Four Commitments

If you want to build a stronger brand-centric company, with more successful launches, you'll need to make these commitments:

1) **Assume** that brand building is not intuitive and you can expedite the process by learning a different methodology. Most highly successful companies conscientiously follow the principles found in this book. You won't have to be lucky or miraculously intuitive to know the path. It is right here, in the pages of this book.

2) **Accept** that you will be skeptical and want to dismiss the examples as "not applicable to my company." But most of them truly do apply. This is business, not personal.

3) **Learn** from the examples and concentrate on how to *adapt* them for your company.

4) **Don't quit**. Becoming a brand-centric company takes practice until it becomes a *natural* part of your thinking. The second biggest mistake, after not starting at all, is giving up *just befo*re you succeed.

The Usual Disclaimers

First, this book contains some *general* legal advice. Your circumstances may differ from the examples in this book, so before you take action, it is always a good idea to have a lawyer who is a specialist in this area (trademark law, not general IP law) review your situation.

Second, this book is a guide to *best practices* in trademarking and branding. It is not intended to teach exceptions and workarounds to the *core* rules because exceptions are not the best practice and are risky. If your legal advisor gives you specific legal advice which is markedly different from statements in this book, it may be an exception specifically relevant to your situation.

The reason for understanding best practices is that they give one room to make small mistakes and still stay on the correct path. Even if you *could* drive on the shoulder of a road, you wouldn't do so without good reason. Look, you have enough business risk to worry about. Deviating from best practices just adds another set of uncertainties.

Chapter 1

Building a *Brand-Centric* Company

(Not a Company with a Brand)

There is a world of difference between a ***brand-centric*** company and a company with a brand. In a brand-centric company, building the brand is part of every business decision. Every sale and every marketing effort builds upon the previous ones, so that over time, the company's *reputation* is infused into its brand. As brand recognition builds, the company has greater sales momentum, and marketing gets easier. If you are a service company, prospects seek out your company's services, and as the brand gets stronger, customers are presold even before they make first contact with your company. In short, the brand precedes and paves the way to the sale.

A brand-centric company will grow faster and can raise its rates or prices because the brand adds value. Surprisingly, even with increased prices, sales won't slow; in fact, they may actually accelerate as the brand-centric company becomes known as the *premier* brand in its field or geographic locale.

On the other hand, for a company *with a brand*, the brand is a necessary address, but otherwise unimportant relative to the putative ideal of business activities: sales and short term profits. In these companies, little thought will go into selecting a name. Typically, this will be done just before incorporation, when the lawyer asks, "What are you going to call it?"

In companies with (simply) a brand, there is a belief that the value of the company is related to 1) the strength of the management team, 2) low prices, and 3) good service.

Of course, sales are vital, as are a great management team, good service, and attractive prices, but these factors alone have limits. The difference between a *brand-centric* company and a company *with a brand* is much like the difference between a home owner and a renter. The renter never accumulates any equity in the rental property and consequently is not motivated to make improvements to increase the property's value. The homeowner, on the other hand, realizes that every improvement will return a double benefit. They get to enjoy the improvement while they live there, and the next buyer will pay part of the cost in an increased valuation.

Similarly, a brand is an investment in the company that also pays back twice. It helps sell today's product, makes the next sale easier, and grows margins. Simultaneously, it makes the company worth much more, either in stock value for public companies or selling price for privately held ones.

Companies claiming to have a brand, but that are not brand-centric, practice *brute force* marketing. Every sale is a full court press. Prior sales successes don't make future sales easier. There is no brand momentum. These companies' owners are working much too hard to achieve the same results realized by brand-centric ones.

When it costs essentially the same to build a brand-centric company as a brute force company with a "sort of" brand begs the question:

Why aren't all companies brand-centric?

Building a brand is not intuitive. It doesn't come naturally to most people, even those with skills in other areas of growing a company. It is a learned process.

Becoming a brand-centric company requires three things:

1. Knowing where your company currently stands with respect to its brand.
2. Accepting that becoming brand-centric is worth the incremental effort and that it is not intuitively obvious.
3. Not quitting, especially just before the company succeeds in becoming brand-centric.

This book will speak to all three of these requirements.

Brand-Centric Companies: Case Studies

Brand-centric companies are stronger, with higher margins, and they have momentum from product to product. The following examples illustrate the vital importance of some famous brands to their companies' success. Even small companies can learn a lot by studying these examples.

Before 1991, Intel was an example of a *company with a brand* that transformed itself, as a matter of survival, into a brand-centric company. Most people have heard of the "intel inside" story, but behind the scenes, there is a lot more to their story, as well as critical lessons for every company.

Intel was about to launch the 486 processor to replace the 386. The 486 was better, faster, and cheaper, but very few end-user customers had ever heard of Intel, and they didn't care what brand of processer was in their computer. What they cared about was the brand name on the computer case: Dell, IBM, Compaq, HP, etc.

Although Intel made the best processor, that R&D came with a problem: Intel's processors were more expensive than their competitors'. Intel had two main competitors in the microprocessor world, AMD and Cyrix, both of which made products that were practically clones of Intel's product. Intel would spend millions of dollars in R&D to create the next processor, and AMD and Cyrix would make very similar versions within the year. The competitive product wasn't identical and indeed the Intel product was superior. But *if no one knew, what was Intel's competitive advantage?*

When computer makers (IBM, Dell, Compaq, etc.) needed processors, they would send their buyers to get the lowest price. Most often that was not Intel.

Computer makers had an ace in the hole: when it came to microprocessors, consumers didn't know what a microprocessor was, so it didn't make any difference to them who made it. If a cheaper processor meant the computer was cheaper, that was just fine.

Intel realized that it needed to take away the computer makers' advantage. The miracle of "intel inside" is that not only did the computer makers give up their most important market advantage, they also unwittingly jumped at the opportunity to do so. Only later did they realize what a mistake they had made, but by then it was too late. Here's how Intel did it.

In the beginning, Intel was just a geeky company no one had ever heard of. It had no brand recognition amongst *end-user* customers; consequently, their market share was being taken by lower-cost competition. If they spent $500 million in R&D developing a new processor, after a while AMD would build a similar product at a lower price. Intel was creating the market, and AMD was eating their lunch.

The change Intel made is the one every successful brand-centric company must make:

From now on, every business decision must have a brand-building component.

Making the best technology doesn't matter if the customer doesn't know enough to care. The brand is there to help customers to care.

Before "intel inside" came along, the hierarchy of brand importance in the PC world had the maker's brands on top, the brand of the operating system next, and the brands of the subcomponents a very distant last.

Desktop brand pyramid circa 1991

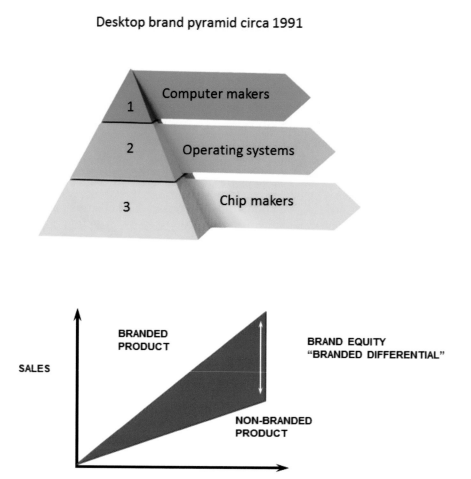

After "intel inside," Intel was the most important brand in PC world. If it didn't have an Intel processor, then for many buyers, the purchase was a non-starter, regardless of the PC maker's brand on the box.

Desktop brand pyramid – Post Intel Inside Campaign

Intel effectively leapfrogged over all computer brands and eliminated most of its microprocessor competition at the same time.

So how did they do it?

It's about (re)alignment, or the *"intel inside" miracle.*

What Intel did, in a nutshell, is it changed, or realigned, the end user/customer's perception of **what a computer is.**

Before "intel inside," the computer maker was the company that made the cabinet, a box that included the computer's "guts."

After "intel inside," the computer was the *microprocessor*, and the computer maker (HP, Dell, etc.) merely made boxes to keep the processor from falling out! In effect, Intel made the computer makers

12

pretty much irrelevant. Buying a computer became all about which processor to buy: Intel or no-name.

It was a miraculous transformation.

So how did they do it, and more importantly, *why didn't the computer makers try to stop them?* This transformation was going to severely damage the value of the computer-makers' brands. Didn't they see this coming?

Intel's strategy was simple but daring. They offered, in co-op advertising dollars, up to 50% of the advertising budget of the computer makers, so long as the computer makers promoted the "intel inside" logo, displayed it prominently, and played the five-note musical jingle (created by Walter Werzowa) on TV or the Internet. Of course, they had to buy some Intel chips, too.

Intel Bong

Note: Intel did not prohibit the computer makers from selling PCs with AMD or Cyrix chips. They just needed to let the public know that the best computer experience was a computer with an Intel chip. That meant any computer (box) was fine so long as it had an Intel processor inside.

Simultaneously, Intel marketed directly to consumers on why an Intel chip assured the best computing experience. They particularly targeted *gamers,* who traditionally lead the market because their need for high-speed graphics is critical to a good game experience.

Impressive performance. Exciting visuals.
Stunning performance starts with an Intel® Core™ i3 processor

Intel's brand-centric business strategy used co-op advertising support as the lubricant to overcome computer-maker resistance. What computer company could resist a 50% co-op advertising payment from Intel? If the computer makers had a Brand Czar whose job it was to protect the brand, they would have flatly refused this deal. Clearly there was no one in charge of *brand* at the computer makers. They thought they were getting advertising support from their geeky parts supplier (Intel). What they actually got was partial destruction of their own brands.

After "intel inside," the realigned perception of a computer looked like this:

The CHIP is the computer.

(The computer makers merely make boxes to prevent the microprocessor chip from falling out.)

Buy *any* computer. Just make sure it has an Intel processor.

As a result, in the desktop market, computer-maker brands became largely irrelevant. If it had an Intel chip and ran Windows, it didn't much matter who made the box.

Why didn't the computer makers see Intel's strategy as the threat it was? There are two plausible answers, both of which are probably right. First: greed. Fifty percent co-op advertising money was too sweet to ignore. Second, lack of a *Brand Czar* at the company's helm. A true brand-centric company has the equivalent of a CBO – Chief Branding Officer, usually the CEO, whose job is to spot and stop evisceration of the brand. If the CBO/CEO is not a brand-centric thinker, "intel inside" happens.

The result was that Intel dominated the processor market, leaving AMD and Cyrix in the dust. Consumers, gamers, and businesses trust Intel. In other words, the brand is *working*.

By the way, this Intel miracle had little effect on one computer maker: Apple. Why?

Apple was on an entirely different brand track. It was not targeting gamers, but graphic artists and students. The Apple brand was then what it still is today: simplicity of use and elegance of appearance. Which microprocessor Apple used was unimportant to its brand. Furthermore, Apple didn't, and actually couldn't, take the co-op money: it was using the Motorola processor, which was completely incompatible with Intel. Eventually, Apple *did* switch to the Intel processor (for Windows compatibility), but its brand was already so strong, few people really noticed the switch from Motorola to Intel.

Another industry may not be as susceptible to being "rewired" in such a dramatic way as the computer industry was after "intel inside," but brand building will still always produce positive results.

There is no need for a marketing genius to find opportunities for brand building. The "intel inside" campaign wasn't an original idea. It was borrowed from the NutraSweet logo program of Monsanto, only Intel's was better executed.

For most companies, brand building is not about investing money in some sort of brand machine. It's about **realignment of efforts, sometimes ever so slightly**, so that every marketing and sales effort builds brand equity. Then, repeat and repeat and repeat. In other words: don't quit.

Just follow this mantra:

> **From now on, every business decision**
>
> **must have a brand-building component.**

In other words, if there isn't a direct *brand benefit* in a business decision, *realign the decision* until there is one. Often this is very easy. The true master will learn to do this with little thought. Until you reach that master level, write the mantra on your wall and look at it often.

Believing in the power of brand-centricity can be a leap of faith at first. It is shocking to realize that some of the most valuable brand-centric companies have virtually no other assets besides their brand.

.

(old logo)

Consider Uber.

As this book was being written, Uber didn't exist. At printing, the company was valued at over $40 billion despite (or perhaps because of) legal challenges to its service around the globe.

What does Uber own?

- Concept? Yes, the *idea* that there was a better way to deliver taxi services.

- Cars? No, they belong to the drivers.

- Drivers (employees)? No, they are independent contractors on commission.

- An "app" (mobile software to link drivers with passengers)? Yes.

- Patent rights sufficient to stop competitors? No.

- Great execution? Yes.

- The Uber brand? Yes!

Taking account of the company's key assets, where could investors find $40B in value? Investors need to know that Uber has sufficient control over the marketplace. This can come in terms of legal barriers to entry (patents, knowhow) or market barriers to entry (trademarks).

In the case of Uber, which already has competitors, the only barrier to entry is **reputation**--there are no dominating patents on the basic concept, the app is inexpensive to replicate, the drivers are all freelancers, the company has competitors like Lyft, Curb, and Sidecar. But when people mention car sharing services, the first name that comes up is *Uber*.

Reputation is public awareness + an association with (positive) attributes. But reputation is *not* a transferable asset. It is termed a "blue sky" asset. It cannot be sold or transferred until it is turned into a legal right. That right is its *registered* trademark: the word Uber and the Uber logo. If one infuses public awareness of Uber and its great reputation for service into the unique and memorable brand – Uber, and its distinctive logo – the value is created.

Before the Uber brand was recognizable, Uber was largely defenseless and valueless. Now, its trademark is substantially its only real barrier to entry. There are no patents on the "Uber process." Anyone can copy Uber's model, but nobody can copy its name or the reputation infused in that name.

Still, is it really worth $40B? Was Facebook® worth $16B, Alibaba $225B, Twitter $25B? Supposing they are all 50% too high, these numbers are still high enough to show that brands are hugely valuable. Google's initial market capitalization was $23B. Its current market capitalization is $360B. Maybe Uber's value is overstated, but this "blue sky," as accountants call it, must be exceedingly valuable or investors would not be willing to pay such huge sums for it. Clearly, ignoring the value of becoming *brand-centric* is a huge mistake.

Here is Uber's formula for success:

$$I + IP + E + T = TV$$

Here are the variables:

I = idea/concept

IP = intellectual property (legal barriers to entry, patents, trademarks, copyrights)

E = (great) execution

T = Time (staying the course--don't quit)

TV = transferable value, i.e., corporate worth

Note: you won't see the L (luck) variable. DL (dumb luck) is likewise not present in this formula. Of course, we all *hope* for luck, even L^2 (luck squared), but luck and hope are not strategies and certainly not brand strategies.

The time variable is very important to understand. Building reputation and brand can be a slow process, not suitable for *short attention term thinking*. Giving up (just) before the brand is truly established is the second biggest mistake of brand building. (The first is not starting at all). With a lot of marketing money, the timeline can be shortened, but if it's done right, just word-of-mouth customer marketing will bring success.

Now, let's apply the formula $I + IP + E + T = TV$ to Uber.

Their **concept** was great. First they identified the problems in their market:

- Traditional taxis have a reputation for being dirty.

19

- Taxi drivers have a reputation for being surly and, in some countries, as many tourists can attest, fraudsters.
- Taxi companies routinely say they have dispatched a taxi when they have not, so there's often a long wait.

Then they created a mechanism to fix the problems:

- An app tells you where your driver's car is on a map, and shows its progress to your site, in real time.
- Drivers use their own personal cars.
- Drivers are rated by the passenger on every trip. If a driver gets a score below 4 of 5 stars, they are banished from the Ubersphere.

Parisian taxis drivers performed a sit down strike to protest Uber by parking their cars in the middle of Paris streets. What does that say about Uber? The taxi lobby is fighting for its life against change. (No doubt the buggy whip manufacturer's association put up a similar fight over the horseless carriage.)

Not only was Uber's **concept** great, its **IP strategy** was smart because Uber can't stop competition through patents, because its business methods are now unpatentable. Uber could have selected a weak and unrecognizable name, like Taxi App, Taxi Phone, iTaxi or NewTaxi, but instead, the Uber name is legally very strong and highly recognizable. They have strong ownership in the name. It is already serving them well.

Uber's **execution** was also great:

- The app works! No software meltdowns.

- Social media spreads the word.

- Customers are delighted and praise the brand.

- Governments and taxi unions protest around the world. Thanks for the free publicity!

- **Time**: Uber is expanding slowly, but their brand *precedes* their entry into new markets. Uber never advertises (if you don't count mass publicity by striking taxi drivers).

- Its reputation has been built up by word of mouth.

- As it expands to new territories, the brand is already well known. Its reputation precedes its arrival, so Uber doesn't need to advertise.

All of this equals **TV (transferable brand value)**: Investors are willing to pay $40B.

Uber is not an isolated case.

Uber's concept solved the problem of a failed taxi system. What about solving the problem of car ownership in urban environments, where there's nowhere to store a car?

Zipcar's tag line is WHEELS WHEN YOU WANT THEM.

Here is it's secret sauce:

- If you only need a car some of the time, rent one some of the time, at a rental location that is close and fast.

- If you have one car but occasionally need a second one, why not rent by the hour?

- Locate Zipcars in local neighborhoods a short walking distance from most customers, and automate the rental check in/out so that no attendant or paperwork is needed.

- Provide insurance and fuel as part of the price so everything is simple.

- Target the prime audience:

    o College students under 25. They can't rent from the majors, and they live in concentrated campuses. Locate the rental sites close to campus.

    o Big-city dwellers who pay a fortune to rent a garage or parking space. Save them the cost of parking and they will spend it on Zipcar.

    o People with two cars but who rarely need both cars at the same time.

- Be cool—be Internet-enabled. Appeal to the target audience (mostly under 40) by allowing customers to:

    o Set up accounts on a web/phone app.

    o Reserve cars by app.

    o Unlock car doors with the web app, keys inside, car ready to roll.

    o Refuel using a gas credit card provided in-car.

This all sounds great. Zipcar was never profitable, but it was heading toward profitability when it was purchased by Avis for $400 million.

AVIS

So again, *what* did Avis buy, and why?

Here is an asset inventory on Zipcar:

Assets:

- Cars – zero. Zipcar doesn't own any. All leased.
- Real estate holdings (i.e., parking lots for cars) – zero. Zipcar doesn't own them, either.
- Computer reservation system and app – yes, Zipcar has one, but so does Avis.
- Employees with special skills – Zipcar has 493 full and part-time employees. Most of the skilled work is in the app (probably outsourced).
- Patents – no patents which dominate the field.
- The Brand – Zipcar. Of course, that is where the money was.

Competitors: Yes, lots. Hertz has Hertz On Demand, Enterprise has Car Share, etc. There appear to be no barriers to entry.

If Hertz and Enterprise could build this business without buying Zipcar's assets, what did Avis get for the $400 million?

First, consider the assets that *weren't* purchased:

- Avis didn't need Zipcar's vehicles. They already get better prices as a volume purchaser of cars, and Zipcar's vehicles (mostly hybrids) just added another type of vehicle to their service headaches.

- Avis didn't need the reservation system. Zipcar's mobile app is good, but Hertz and Enterprise had no problem replicating it.

Clearly Avis bought the brand, and only the brand, for $400M. They got immediate access to the cohort of Zipcar renters, and it's a good bet those Zipcar renters will grow up to be Avis renters. Basically, Avis was buying its future relationship to younger drivers and city dwellers.

Brand Differential

Brand differential is in action every day, but as consumers, we don't often notice it (or don't want to notice it). Luxury goods are the most blatant example. Compared to their poorer mid-market cousins, luxury goods retail at prices that are often 10x higher, yet their material and labor costs are never close to this 10x multiple. It is pure profit.

A mid-level pair of women's shoes might sell for $150-200. A low-end shoe could be $50. The luxury brand, Prada, could easily cost $1000+. (Yes, $1K is hardly the most expensive, but it's too scary to think of what the upper limit could be). So, the high- to low-end differential is about 20x.

The distribution channel for Prada is a lot longer than for Payless (Fioni brand), so there are a lot more people with their hands in your pocket if you buy Prada, though this still doesn't account for the 10 to 20x differential.

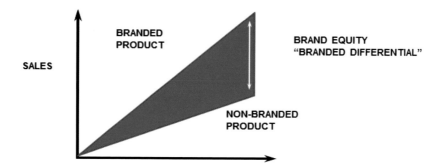

The difference in the quality of the materials, workmanship, and styling between the two brands is significant too, but again, these factors can't make up for the astronomical differential in price. When all **objective** reasons are taken into account, only one factor is left: **brand differential**.

If you are a B to B (business to business) company, be careful not to miss the point being illustrated here. While these examples are Business to Consumer (B to C) channels, the exact same process goes on with B to B marketing; it is just a bit more subtle. If you "exempt" yourself from being brand-centric because you are a B to B company, you are simply exempting yourself from the *benefit* of brand and surrendering to your competitors.

While a company is unlikely to get a 20x differential, getting 1.5x is a big victory, especially if all it requires is a change in decision making. Remember the mantra:

From now on,

every business decision must have a brand-building component.

In short, if there can be a significant increase in price due to being a brand-centric company and having brand recognition, who wouldn't do it?

But I don't sell products!

Of course all of this applies to *service* businesses, too.

Consider a fictitious "Ms. Smith" who works for Accenture doing consulting work. The Accenture hourly rate includes her salary and profits to be distributed to the Accenture partners or shareholders.

Ms. Smith breaks off from Accenture and opens up her consultancy next door to the Accenture office. Can she command the same hourly rate as when she was at Accenture? Except for her current customer(s), she will likely have to cut her hourly rate. Why? Did she become less knowledgeable or less skilled? Obviously not.

Accenture is very brand-centric. Clients come to Accenture because of its reputation more than for its individual employees. Accenture intends to keep it that way. It's great to have superstars like Ms. Smith, but at the end of the day, when building a brand-centric company, it's important that customers are coming for the company's reputation. If that means they get Ms. Smith, great, but Accenture makes sure that they have a dozen more like her if she leaves.

If Ms. Smith understands how the Accenture model works, she will obviously try to replicate it. Otherwise, she could make the mistake of building a ME company, which is a company with a brand, and not brand-centric (see next chapter).

Brands Create Momentum

There is a second way in which brands create value for companies: they create momentum. That is, they accumulate prior brand-building efforts, which makes the next sale easier.

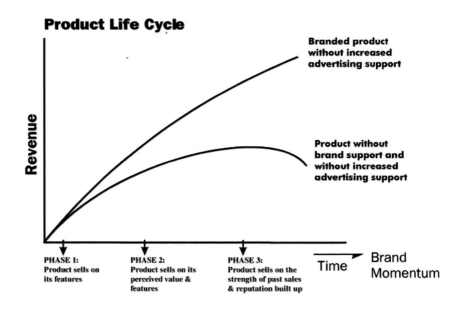

Product Life Cycle

Revenue

Branded product
without increased
advertising support

Product without
brand support and
without increased
advertising support

PHASE 1:
Product sells on
its features

PHASE 2:
Product sells on its
perceived value &
features

PHASE 3:
Product sells on the
strength of past sales
& reputation built up

Time

Brand
Momentum

A simple and obvious example is the momentum Coca-Cola has built up. Coke has a marketing budget of well over $4 billion. That equates to $8,000/minute. If Coke wants to throw a really nice party for the staff in the Atlanta office and they need $250,000 to do it right, they will need to divert their marketing budget expenditure by 30 minutes to siphon off that revenue.

Amazingly, on this fictional planet, Coke approves the diversion and has its holiday bash. Monday morning, back at Coke headquarters, what will happen to sales as a result of this diversion? Will sales drop, now, later, *ever*, as a result? What if Coke threw a big, world-wide party, spent $1 billion, and also gave every Coke employee a new pair of Pradas? Would that show up in the bottom line? Yes, eventually, but slowly and far less damaging than if there was no Coke brand momentum. It is no accident that 150 years of brand momentum pays them back every day.

Both brand differential and brand momentum are common-sense concepts. They don't cost more to implement, and they are as magical as compound interest. If your company hasn't fully implemented an effective brand strategy, it's leaving a lot of money on the table.

In brand-centric companies, the brand is the largest asset (and yet it's off the books).

From an accounting point of view, brand value doesn't exist. Don't be fooled by arcane accounting rules. Even the latest IRS accounting rules do not count the value of a brand unless the brand was purchased. So, by accounting's standards, the Coke brand shows up as a ZERO on the balance sheet.

The Coca-Cola Company owns very few production/bottling facilities. That work is done by independent contractors/franchises. Coke has relatively few hard assets – just some buildings around the world and syrup concentrate manufacturers. However, it owns many brands.

Most of Coke's products have many competitors and are products not difficult to make: mostly sweetener and water. In the case of Dasani®, just water.

So, if zero value were assigned to the brand, how can the Coca-Cola Company be worth $200 billion?

If its value is in its *profitability*, then the question is, how profitable would it be *without* its hundreds of famous brands? The answer, of course, is vastly less. Consider this test: market a bottle of unbranded water adjacent to a bottle of Dasani® (or better yet, Fiji® water), at the same price. Which is going to sell better? The two products are technically identical: filtered water in a bottle. Dasani will either sell better, sell for more, or both. How much cheaper does the unbranded water have to be to take all Dasani® sales away? That is also a measure of the value of the brand.

One might say that the reason Dasani® sells better is that it has been advertised, implying that the brand has accumulated value from advertising and retains that value. As to the generic bottled water, what value does it retain?

While appraising exact brand value is always difficult, it is far from impossible. In public companies, the stock price, over the long term, is a very good measure of brand value.

Where does your company fit into this brand continuum?

Does your company have a good *reputation* in its industry, community, or amongst customers? If the answer is yes, then it's half of the way to being a brand-centric company. What is left is to *transform that reputation into a brand that makes it valuable, ownable, and transferable.*

Without the **transformation** from reputation to brand, there won't be any momentum or price differential.

Avoiding Extinction: Disruptive Change

Brands confer enhanced profits and momentum, but they can also *save* a company from extinction by providing a buffer to *disruptive change*.

Even the most hardened of brand skeptics should care about disruptive change. Disruptive change is something that *eliminates* a business or industry. Often you can't see it coming, and you can't plan for it. This sort of rapid radical change is happening a lot, but it is not a new phenomenon. Back in the day, the carriage manufacturers thought they had a lifetime lock on the business. Then, poof.

Consider some newer technologies that are likely next on the chopping block:

Land line telephones

Replaceable, cheap incandescent light bulbs

Computer printers

Blackberry phones

Newspapers/printed magazines

Bookstores

Typewriters

Fax machines

Wrist watches (except as jewelry or as smart phone extenders)

Keys

Credit cards

Paper money/coins

Nowadays, disruptive change happens much faster than in horse-carriage days. Ask Blackberry.

And consider the evolution of Uber. Suppose it's 2011 and you just paid $1 million for an NYC taxicab medallion. Uber started in 2012 and got big within 24 months. Despite all efforts to fight Uber, the taxi business is going to change. If you own the Yellow taxi cab company, you should be working on leveraging your brand to outperform Uber instead of trying to fight it.

Amazon started in 1986. It sold books. It killed the bookstore business. It now sells everything. Whose retail business is next?

Alibaba is 100x bigger than Amazon. Who can predict what it will do?

Disruptive change is an equal opportunity category killer. It kills both weak and strong businesses, *but brand-centric businesses have built-in survival plans.* Consider the example of Dolby Labs.

How Dolby Labs survived disruptive change

Dolby Labs should be dead and buried. It's not. What's more, it is the biggest name in digital sound recordings in the movie industry.

▶◀ **DOLBY.**

In the 60s, Dolby Labs solved a vexing problem in the sound industry.

Remember analog audio tapes, i.e., cassette tapes? They were pocket-sized, but the tape was very narrow, so the sound quality was very poor. The metal tape scraping across a metal recording head created a hissing background sound. This was okay for rock music, but otherwise annoying.

Along came (Sir) Ray Dolby, who miraculously solved the problem merely by designing a clever circuit to suppress the hiss.

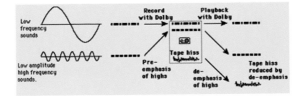

From an engineer's point of view, it was a very counter-intuitive solution, but it saved the cassette tape industry and made Dolby Labs mountains of money. Dolby Labs got many patents and thoroughly protected its brand, but it could not have anticipated what would happen next.

Digitized sound. A new technology which is completely clear of static, noise, and hiss. When you listen to an orchestral recording, during a musical pause there is no background noise *at all* other than occasional coughs and sneezes from the audience. (Dolby is probably working on that also.) This was great news for sound purists, but wasn't it the end of the line for Dolby Labs? In other words, if Dolby solved the hiss problem of analog recordings, but digital recordings have no hiss at all, shouldn't Dolby be superfluous?

No. Long before the end of analog audio, Dolby realized that its value to the world must be more than solving the *analog* problem. Dolby turned its R&D to other sound problems in digital recording and created innovative solutions a second time. Dolby became the premier technology company *by making all audio sound better.*

Perhaps most important to their success, they sold the movie industry on the idea that *if it had sound, it needed Dolby.* Then they sold the public on the idea that a movie, which had DOLBY sound, was going to be an amazing experience. The Dolby brand is emblazoned on all movie advertising (very reminiscent of "intel inside").

Disruptive change does not disrupt a company whose brand positioning *rises above* the technology that died.

Compare two possible brand *positions* for Dolby:

A. We remove the hiss in analog sound.

B. We make *everything* you hear sound better.

They chose plan B. **Plan B can only be disrupted if we revert to silent movies again.**

Common sense would dictate that Dolby would have disappeared with analog audio. Instead, Dolby is now the number one company in sound enhancement; there is hardly a movie or sound production that doesn't proudly display the Dolby Digital logo.

Remember: **disruptive change never announces itself**.

Being brand-centric allows a company to be much more resilient in the midst of disruptive change.

Takeaways for this chapter:

1. Brand-centric companies are fundamentally different from companies that claim to have a brand but haven't really invested in building a brand. To be brand-centric, a company must live the mantra, **"From now on, every business decision must have a brand-building component."**

2. Pick the reason you prefer to build a brand-centric business (any will do):

    a. Higher margins

    b. Momentum from sale to sale

    c. Defense against disruptive change

3. The formula for building a brand applies to all companies, all sizes, all of the time.

4. *Thinking* a business is brand-centric is much like *hoping* to succeed. Hoping is not a strategy.

5. Be honest in evaluating how much true investment your company has made in becoming brand-centric. You can't fix it if you can't acknowledge the problem.

Chapter 2

IT'S ALL ABOUT

ME

The Curse of the ME Company

Why profitable, privately held companies are often *unsalable*

This chapter is dedicated to CEOs running very successful companies, with $5-100M in revenues. This group constitutes about 95% of all North American businesses. It's also the group that has the most to gain from this book and may well be the most resistant to making the changes needed to be brand-centric. It also has the most to lose, since most privately held business owners have most of their wealth tied up in their company.

Here's a warning:

Even though a business is profitable, there is a very good chance that it is unsalable.

In North America, about 60-70% of privately held businesses are owned by people in their 50s-70s. Typically, these owners have given very little thought to their transition/exit, yet most are within 10 years or less, of an orderly or, more likely, a forced transition. When it does happen, and it surely will, it will not be pretty. The vast majority of these businesses are largely unsalable except as "residual value," i.e., the value of the building and land. The owners don't realize this because they don't know what they don't know. *A profitable business is not necessarily saleable.*

For a business to be saleable, it must have something the *buyer* wants. It's critical to see the transaction **through the eyes of the buyer**. What they are looking for is very different from what most privately held businesses have to offer.

This problem is known as

The ME Company Dilemma.

The ME company is one that was started by a powerful founder, who, by skill, savvy, hard work, luck, and most importantly, *personality*, built a business from nothing. Such companies are entitled to be proud of their accomplishments. They are an impressive group.

What makes them so successful is often the same thing that makes them vulnerable to the ME company dilemma. Their weakness is that they don't realize that the company's greatest strength, themselves, can *never* be a transferable asset. If you find yourself in this group, please understand that your accomplishment is considerable, but until you convert your company to being brand-centric, it is unsalable.

This is urgent!

It's obvious why these business owners don't see the urgency of the situation. As a group, they are highly motivated people who don't *ever* plan to stop working. They probably don't need the money, but they like (love) the challenge of their CEO role. They've done it for so long that they don't know what they would do if they stopped working. (No one can play golf *every* day, can they?) If they don't plan to ever quit working, and the economy needs them, then where's the urgency?

There's a *New Yorker* cartoon where a life insurance salesman is just closing a deal with a client on a life insurance policy. The client has one last question before he signs the papers. He asks, "But what happens if I don't die?"

If these CEOs don't see themselves retiring any time soon, again, what is the urgency? It is this: the motivation to sell will come in more subtle and compelling ways. Some may want to live in a warmer climate, or near their children or grandchildren, or they may have a close call with a health issue that forces them to recognize their mortality. They realize: *I am not going to live forever. Why am I still working for money I don't need?* Motivation may come from family crises as well. It only takes one to move the mountain.

There will *always* be something. Founders in their 20s and 30s already know that they are going to sell their business, but they are also just as likely to have created a ME company as their older brethren. They have more time to fix it, but time flies when you are busy running a business.

What happens next is critical.

Suppose that, for whatever reason, the decision is made to sell the company and start a new life. At this point, the sale of the business would, ideally, be completed in 6-12 months.

The business is very profitable, so it may be assumed that it will be an easy sale and there will be a juicy second payday in the form of a big cash payment. The accountant will state that the business is in top form, has good financials, and it should sell quickly for a multiple of earnings.

But as potential buyers start to poke around the company, they'll be asking unexpected questions. What they're doing is called Due Diligence. It's a lot like looking under the bed for dust bunnies. *All* of the dust bunnies.

In my practice, I do a lot of these due-diligence analyses, mostly for buyers. (Sellers are often sitting ducks and totally unprepared.) Concentrating on intellectual property, I get called in to these acquisitions quite late in the process, so the deal price is usually already set. Nevertheless, I always ask the buyer if they would like to pay *less*. They are always surprised by the question. I tell them that there is always (not *almost* always) a skeleton in the closet that will slash the value of the company. It may even kill the deal, but it will certainly cause the buyer to adjust their offer. It's not that I am especially skilled at due diligence, but that I know where to look.

Here's what I'm telling you: what I will find wrong with the business can be fixed, but not in a month or a year. It will take several years. So, if you're reading this and you aren't already selling, then I am just in time.

Why ME Companies are Unsalable

What buyers want to know is simple:

What assets can I acquire and own?

In other words, what will be *left* after the founder leaves?

Chapter 1 was about how a brand will often be a company's most valuable asset. Brand value is easy to see when it applies to *Fortune 500* companies. If you are the owner/founder of a privately held business, you may naturally believe that the rules of branding don't apply to smaller companies like yours. You would be wrong.

The law of branding, like the law of gravity, works the same for every company. No one is exempt.

If you ignore building a true brand-centric company, you are likely handing your competitor an open invitation to take your place as the brand leader in your market.

In a hypothetical future sale of a ME business, the value of the brand is really the *person* who made the company what it is. Denying this sets the founder up for very painful and shocking consequences. Consider the following scenario:

Accenture is a true branding success story because they have overcome, as much as one can, the greatest problem in personal services companies: scalability. They have figured out how to grow by hiring new, smart people, out of top universities, who really come with few skills or knowledge useful to Accenture. They take these newbie grads and make them capable of billing at $200-1,200/hr advising big companies. What they do is not magic. They have a few really skilled people at the top, a huge database of prior knowledge, and they rely on the newbies to access that data and learn fast (hence the top universities). It's a difficult learning curve, but Accenture has cracked the code on scalability and has a real market advantage.

Continuing our fantasy: after a few years at Accenture, you leave and strike out on your own. Over time your consulting field narrows to, say, environmental compliance. It's a growing field. You have learned a lot from your prior experience and you are ready to launch your own business.

You quickly form an LLC for your consultancy firm. Just as you are walking out of the lawyer's office, the lawyer asks, "What do you want to call your company? I need to check with the Secretary of State to see if the name is available." You hadn't thought much about it, but you know you want to pick a name that helps your launch. Something that will help clients know *immediately* what you do. You decide on *The Environmental Consultants*, LLC. The Secretary of State search clears and you are incorporated. (More on the relative meaninglessness of this search clearance later.)

Because of your inner strength, drive, engaging personality, and a ton of long hours learning from Accenture, you are successful. Indeed, the name of the company made it easy for prospects to find you. Consulting is a person-to-person business, so you quickly reach your limits of capacity and hire more consultants. Following the Accenture model, you hire young, smart people who can learn fast. That also means you need to do a lot of one-on-one coaching since you don't have the database of knowledge that Accenture has. Over time, your hires come and go, and you lose some clients on their departure. That hurts, so you decide that your solution is to be closely involved with every client in every deal. You may not be doing much of the work, but the clients see *you* as *their* man/woman, and frankly, you like it.

(You have just made your first ME mistake. Did you see it? But let's continue...)

As a consequence, now when a hire leaves the company, you rarely lose business. Clients know that *you* ultimately stand for the quality of the company, and they are very happy.

Fast forward 35 years. You've made a lot of money and you have come to terms with the sale of your business, which should be worth a lot because you have huge margins – anyone would salivate at the chance to scoop those up.

Or would they?

Obviously the facts are exaggerated to make the point, but only a little. A similar story could be told about a manufacturing business, parts supply distributor, restaurant, and so on.

Now let's walk through the value of the business from **the founder's** point of view.

The Environmental Consultants, LLC:

Annual revenues: high

Margins: very high

Clients: 75% of the business is through three anchor clients; therwise many smaller ones

Prospect for industry growth: very good

Number of key employees with skills to handle clients alone: 5

Non-compete agreements: none (these may be illegal in some states)

Number of equity partners: none

Office space: rented

Asking price: 5x gross revenues

Assume there is an out-of-town investor who owns a number of environmental consulting agencies in other cities and wants an anchor in your city.

Here's what the **buyer** sees:

You are the company.

The brand (The Environmental Consultants) is worthless for three reasons: 1) it is not protectable as a brand, 2) you don't own it: you never registered it with the US Patent and Trademark Office (FYI: the Secretary of State registration you have on your corporate name is meaningless and does not give you ownership), and 3) your clients don't come to you because of the company brand, but because of YOU. In other words, you are a ME company with a brand, a brand which you don't properly own and can't sell.

In later chapters, reasons 1 and 2 will be dealt with in detail. For now, let's focus on reason 3.

You didn't build a brand-centric company. You are a company with a brand, but the real brand is <u>you</u> no matter what the sign on the door says. The clients love you, but *you* are leaving. They don't love your company. They don't *know* anything about your company, they don't know what your company stands for, and they don't know what makes the company unique and desirable – except that they like *you*.

Instead of becoming brand-centric, you became ME-centric. You knew every client, and they loved you. Problem is, **you are not for sale.** Your company also has an ineffective and unprotectable name (Chapters 4 and 5 will further discuss brand names and ownership). It is not a brand. It is hollow. Again, the company's only real value is *you*.

Continuing with the story, another buyer appears and sees that you have three anchor clients and five key employees. They make you an offer of 1x earnings, which you reject, and they walk.

During the due diligence process, which turns over every document ever written, it leaks out to the key employees that the company is for sale. Three of them jump ship to a competitor and win over two of your company's anchor clients because they tell these clients that you are going to fold up soon anyway. Now there is little or nothing to sell.

The 5x you wanted for the business was *always* an illusion. You weren't prepared because you built a ME company instead of building a company with *transferable value*. Transferable value is created by transferring your reputation into a brand and focusing all efforts on building the brand, not just your personal reputation.

The following story is about a real company. The name can't be revealed, but it could easily have been your company. It is was a ME company, but it became a brand-centric company that was ultimately sold for 2.5x of what the owner originally asked for – to the *same* buyer.

This **ME** company was, by all business measures, successful – it was profitable, held good market share, had instant name recognition of the **ME** founder/owner and enjoyed a solid reputation in its field. After 20 years of being tirelessly immersed in every facet of the business, the exhausted owner of the ME company decided he would like to sell his business and retire to the tropics.

At first blush, our ME company looked ripe for acquisition, and indeed it received the interest of an acquirer. The ME company figured it was worth $4 million based on sales, profits, and its brand.

Unfortunately, the brand was entirely bound up with the personality of Mr./Ms. ME, who was a forceful, intense, and dynamic personality. Great qualities, but utterly non-transferable.

Although his company had an enviable client list, solid reputation for good candidates, and strong and growing revenue, the potential buyer informed him that there was "nothing to buy" except a storefront lease in that city and a client list. The ME company had no processes in place for expansion, and no marketing or sales collateral pieces existed apart from business cards. All of the outside client relationships were only established with the founder, Mr. ME, and no one else in the company. Every single facet of this company's identity was tied to its ME owner. Nothing about the firm was brand-centric. Yet, the company was highly profitable, so he was dumbfounded by the acquirer's statement that there "was nothing to buy."

Mr. ME was devastated when the potential acquirer explained the branding problem and then walked without making any kind of offer, except for some important advice: Become a *real* company, where the brand is not YOU, and we'll talk again.

Mr. ME was lucky. He was given critical knowledge. He was also smart. He didn't fall back on ego and reject the knowledge. He used it.

The ME company changed every aspect of the business to strengthen the brand and minimize his personal importance.

It took him four years to fix a problem which had existed for twenty.

The prospective acquiring company noticed the change and came back to make him a new offer. This time it was $10 million. He took it. He can be reached at his new address in the Caribbean. Lucky guy. He got a second chance. Imagine what his company might have been worth had he had that knowledge when he started the company.

Many years ago, McGraw Hill ran this peculiar ad. They probably didn't realize that they had created the perfect ad for why ME companies are so dangerous.

The text in the ad below reads:

> I don't know who you are.
> I don't know your company.
> I don't know your company's product.
> I don't know what your company stands for.
> I don't know your company's customers.
> I don't know your company's record.
> I don't know your company's reputation.
> Now — what was it you wanted to sell me?

This is the essence of the unbranded ME company dilemma. Your company is highly successful, yet it is essentially unsalable except for hard assets, like real estate. The problem is that your day-to-day success *masks* the underlying hollow core, sapping your motivation to fix the problem before it is too late.

So, even if only a small part of this story applies to your company, it's important to take action now.

Takeaways for this chapter:

1. It is never too late to become brand-centric.

2. It can't be done overnight. It may take some years, but starting is critical.

3. Denying that there is a problem is the default for most small companies. Profitability masks the underlying problem, but it will be revealed at sale.

4. Brand-centric companies inherently grow fast and are more profitable, so you will benefit even now by becoming brand-centric.

Chapter 3

Brand Positioning

Why the first step to brand building is *not* picking a brand

It would seem that the way to begin the process of becoming a brand-centric company is by focusing on *the brand*. Yet, surprisingly, that would be the wrong approach. Starting with the brand is the equivalent of following a recipe from the middle to the end, skipping the first steps. If it worked, it would be dumb luck.

Brand positioning, aka strategic positioning, is the definition of *what your brand stands for and why a customer should care.* It is a step that is often skipped because, as has been mentioned, building a brand-centric company is not an intuitive skill – it has to be learned. But the first (and probably the hardest) step to learn is not to skip this step.

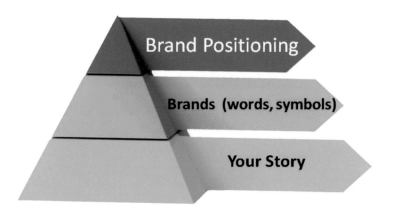

What is often not understood about brands is this: brands are merely the *carriers* of the company's story, i.e., they position the company in relation to its customers. They are a *shorthand* way to encapsulate a company's relationship with its customers in very few words.

Your company's *positioning* needs to be what you want the customer to think about your company when they consider buying your product/service, and even more importantly, how they *feel* about your company *after* purchase. If your brand develops a deeper connection with its customers, they will more easily be enticed back for your next product or service. Remember brute-force marketing, i.e., marketing with no brand? Every sale is hard. A well-positioned brand has the opposite effect. Marketing becomes far easier and less expensive.

The Positioning Test

A quick way to confirm whether your company has any positioning at all is to do the following test:

> Imagine you are just leaving a party. As you step into the elevator, and as the doors close, someone you met at the party darts in with you. You don't really know him/her beyond a

prior hello and handshake. He/she turns to you and says, "So, what is it your company does?"

Yes, it's the elevator speech. You have seven seconds to say something. First, do you actually have something in mind for just this situation? Second, what are you going to say?

If you don't know precisely what should be said in those seven seconds, it is quite likely your company has no positioning. If you *do* have something in mind, but it comes out as essentially, *We are faster/better/cheaper at doing X*, there is an equally good chance that your positioning is not working.

There is a second part to this test: if you asked your partners/colleagues/employees to take this very same test, would they give a nearly identical elevator speech? If not, it is almost certain that the company, as a whole, has no viable positioning – no unified, unique recognizable attribute that makes the company different from all its competitors.

The elements of a great brand position are:

1. Plausibility (i.e., that the company can deliver)
2. Brevity (seven words or less)
3. Relevancy (the customer will care)
4. Depth (it reaches beyond faster, better, cheaper)
5. Endurance (it will outlive the current product line)

What does great positioning look like?

First, a few examples of companies with very clear positions:

It is likely that everyone in North America knows the positioning of Volvo. Safety. Yet it wasn't always so. Back in the 60s, Volvo's positioning in the US was muddled. Somewhere between ugly and overpriced. Now Volvo has complete clarity.

BMW, likewise, has a very clear positioning. "The Ultimate Driving Machine," i.e., engineering.

So, who has the better brakes? And how would you, as their CEO, demonstrate this braking power?

Surprise – for the most part, the cars have basically the same brakes, often made by the same brake supplier.

Yet from a positioning point of view, there is a huge difference between the two brands.

For Volvo, braking is central to safety, so it needs to promote its brakes as effective.

In the case of BMW, as the *ultimate driving machine*, of course it *has* brakes, but the idea is not to emphasize them. After all you won't often need them because you will be able to sprint around the road hazard.

The two companies take the same features and portray them completely differently. That's positioning.

What is critical is that Volvo needs to be a performance vehicle, but if it ever promotes performance over safety, it will lose its soccer mom customer base. If BMW starts emphasizing safety over performance, it will alienate its customer base. Although every once in a while such a thing happens, the company Brand Czar usually pulls the company back from the brink before it gets out of hand.

Similarly, when one walks into one of these two big boxes, it is immediately apparent how they are positioned differently.

> Wal-Mart: Always cheaper. You don't have to comparison shop. When they cut their supplier's prices, they pass some of that on to you. If you spend less, you can buy more stuff.

> Target: Bright, clean stores, well kept, cool designs you wouldn't expect at a big box, not nearly as cheap as Wal-Mart but still affordable. In other words, cheaper but still chic.

They may be competing for the same customers, but not all the time. A customer looking to buy mass quantities of the cheapest paper towels is probably better off at Wal-Mart, but when buying lawn chairs, dishes, or clothing, that same customer will find more interesting stuff at Target. Target is trying to get part of Wal-Mart's customer base by getting them in the store for cooler clothing and then selling them somewhat higher-priced paper towels. If the customer values cool over rock bottom prices, Target wins, because that customer will spend bigger money on dishes at Target and overpay a bit for paper towels. In a recession, Wal-Mart wins; in good times, Target has the advantage. Since Target doesn't have the buying power of Wal-Mart, it can't win the price game, and therefore has to be *positioned* differently. During recessions, Target tends to lose its focus and wander in the low price tar pit, but it usually regains its brand sanity (positioning) and reverts to its strengths.

.

Of course, Apple is the poster child of great brand positioning. Though they never mention it explicitly, every product announces the company's position loud and clear:

When you buy any Apple product, it will be beautiful and easy to use.

It is amazing how the other computer companies have failed to compete with Apple on its basic positioning. When one looks at a MacBook Air, one can only marvel at its sleek look and ease of use. Sure, we know it can crunch numbers, but isn't it beautiful. Do you recall Apple ever mentioning faster, better, or cheaper? Clearly Apple isn't cheaper. Ask Samsung. Samsung out-produces Apple every year in smart phones. Yet it makes far less money per unit. As a company, which would you prefer to be? More profitable or just bigger?

Apple ensures that every single product it makes will be easy to use. The Apple OS has set the standard which Windows spent years trying to catch. There also is a huge difference between iOS (the iPhone operating system) and Android. Every app that runs on iPhone must be cleared by Apple. One of its primary requirements is uniformity – which buttons do what. In other words, Apple insists that all apps be easy to use and more or less uniform. Android has no such review system. It is the Wild West of apps. Not a major problem, but it doesn't follow Apple's mantra of easy-to-use.

This matters. When Apple convinces you that the Mac is easy to use, then you have confidence that their other products (iPod, iPhone, iPad) will be the same. The customer base doesn't doubt for a moment that the other products from Apple will be true to the company's message. That's *positioning.*

Note that neither Apple nor Volvo nor Target ever directly mentions their positioning. The positioning statement is for internal use.

Instead, most companies use their *tagline* as a way to help their customers recognize this positioning. If their positioning is working, ultimately they don't really need the help of a tagline. Apple's positioning is so well understood, they don't mention it.

Getting From Nowhere to the Perfect Brand Positioning

Great positioning is perhaps the hardest marketing challenge there is. There are mountains of books on the subject. One favorite is *Positioning: The Battle for Your Mind,* by Ries and Trout.

In the meantime, here is a shortcut to getting to a great positioning statement. Basically, work backwards, starting with the tagline.

Taglines can get you there.

A great *tagline* can be a very compressed version of a brand positioning statement. It is for public consumption, so it has to be short and concise. That's its virtue. It instantly forces one to concentrate on what matters. Fast.

Sometimes, it is easier to work from a tagline to a full positioning statement. Everyone understands the importance of a tagline, so you will find little resistance within an organization to having one. However, most are created for the wrong reason, by the wrong people within the company. This is very, very important stuff and cannot be delegated to low-level employees. Many people associate positioning statements with mission statements, and it is well known that mission statements are perceived as not worth the e-paper they are printed on.

It is much easier to start with a tagline. That does not mean it is easy to generate a great tagline, but it lowers the barrier to success.

Here is some help – the same rules for positioning apply to taglines, with a few extra requirements:

> No lofty fluff, please (i.e., meaningless statements).

> After 7-10 words, no one is listening.

Remember the basic rules:

1. Plausibility
2. Brevity (short enough)
3. Relevancy
4. Depth (beyond faster, better, cheaper)
5. Differentiation (is it different, and do they care?)
6. Endurance (will it last?)

Consider this cautionary tale about how *not* to do it:

"Nokia – Connecting People"

> Plausible: Sure, but so do two Dixie® cups and a string connect two people.

53

Short enough: Yes.

Relevant: Not really. For a phone company, "connecting people" is considered an entry-level requirement. It's like saying, "Our phones work."

Reaches deep into customer: Hardly.

Differentiation: Nope. Don't all phones do that?

Enduring: Yes, it will always be true.

Even though "Connecting People" is absolutely true, relevant on some level, and enduring, it fails the most important test: connecting with the mind of the customer. "Connecting People" is a basic attribute of all mobile phones. How does Nokia speak to the customer in a unique way, so they will come back?

Did you know that Nokia was the creator of the first truly smart phone, way ahead of Blackberry and Apple? Did you know that Nokia is responsible for most of the technology in the cell towers that makes cell phones work? Nokia's customers might have been interested in knowing this about the company, but they sure don't get it with "Connecting People."

By the way, when Microsoft bought the company, they left the tagline behind.

"Choose freedom. TOSHIBA"

This is not a 4th of July, Independence Day theme. It was about Toshiba's laptop line. The "freedom" was lightweight, powerful laptops. Did you get it? Didn't think so.

HITACHI
Inspire the Next

"Hitachi: Inspire the Next."

If you got Toshiba's tagline, this one should be a cinch. The coolest part is the red accent over the "t."

But, just tell us, next *what*?

Now, here are examples of companies that got it right:

"Raid: Kills Bugs Dead"

This is a superb tagline, albeit it's grammatically absurd. In fact, that is what makes it great.

Let's face it, we all hate bugs, at least in our house. We want them killed. How do we want them killed? Dead. Yes, we want them killed dead, or *double dead*. That is because we hate them so much. Stupid? Not at all.

55

Plausible: Very.

Short enough: Three words!

Relevant: Right on. Did they mention *DEAD*?

Reaches deep into customer: *Absolutely*. We want bugs so dead that we want them double dead. It reaches our innermost loathing of bugs. So, if Raid kills bugs dead, perhaps the competitors don't kill bugs as dead as Raid does. Crazy? Not in the context of bugs.

Differentiation: Yes, if they own "double dead." If any other insecticide brand used a similar tag line, aside from being trademark infringement, it would only reinforce the Raid brand. It doesn't matter whether it makes sense as long as we feel good about it.

Enduring: Sure. If Raid keeps killing bugs dead, we will keep buying Raid.

"Michelin. Because so much is riding on your tires."

Tires: they are the boring black things that prevent the car from scraping the ground. And they wear out fast. Michelin told us that good tires are central to our safety and then added babies into the mix (why not puppies, too?).

Any tire company could have connected tire safety to babies, but Michelin got there first and now owns it. Michelin is also the expert in racing tires. They could have said that, but then it would have destroyed their safety position. Michelin has another position for the racing market, but it has chosen safety for its core market.

"De Beers: A Diamond Is Forever"

Few people know that diamond wedding rings are an invention of De Beers. After World War II, De Beers had more diamonds than it had buyers. It targeted the rich American market to convince couples that diamonds = better marriage. It worked. Diamonds are still not commonly used in wedding bands in Europe or elsewhere. Not because of cost, but because they didn't get the De Beers message.

> *Plausible*: Yes, if one is concerned about stones wearing out, though it is also a double entendre.
>
> *Short enough*: Yes, four words.

Relevance: marriage = forever, (at least that's the plan).

Reaches deep into customer: Absolutely. We all want marriages to last as long as diamonds, so why not send that message?

Differentiation: Not needed. They are selling generic rocks. They control the market. They don't care about competition, just selling more rocks.

Enduring: Sure.

"TED (Technology Entertainment Design): Ideas worth spreading"

We all thought TED was some. In fact it's a collection of recordings of interesting speeches on a zillion topics, which pretty much have nothing in common except they are ideas of such importance that you will want to tell others to watch them.

Plausible: Yes.

Short enough: Yes, two words.

Relevance: TED is *all* about ideas.

Reaches deep into customer: Absolutely. Once you see a few, you will want to tell others to watch.

Differentiation: Yes, from other podcasts of lesser intelligence.

Enduring: Sure. This tagline says, "We will ensure that *all* of our speeches are worthy."

"Servpro: Like it never even happened"

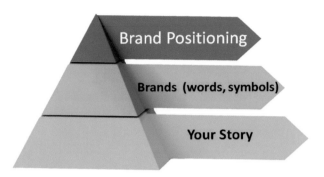

This is the best of the bunch and the one that can teach you the most. This is not a mega company, so it may be easier for some to relate to.

Notice the original tagline: "Fire & Water - Cleanup & Restoration." Yup, that is what Servpro does. Now look at their new tagline: "Like it never even happened."

Say you are considering two cleanup companies for your sewer backup (yuck). Which one gets into the deepest, darkest recesses of your brain? "We do cleanup, m'am," or "When we are done, you can completely forget the experience." Do they have your attention?

> *Plausible*: Yes. If they are really conscientious, they will do a thorough job. Isn't that exactly what you want?

> *Relevance*: Backed up sewers are ugly. Erasing your memory…ahh.

> *Short enough*: Yes, five words.

> *Reaches deep into customer*: It doesn't get much deeper. Sewer backup—awful. Servpro promises that Scotty will beam the mess out to that planet with those Tribbles. Would that be far enough away, ma'am?

> *Differentiation*: Yes, Servpro owns that deep connection to its customer. Notice that they could have chosen "faster, better, cheaper", but it would led to a death struggle with the next

faster, better, cheaper competitor. The best the competition can do now is say, "We do that too."

Enduring: Sure. As long as there are sewers, floods, and tornadoes, we want to forget it ever happened.

Even a small company can crack the positioning code. Create a tagline, and then a position will endure in what totally matters to the customer. It is not faster, better, cheaper – it is beyond all of that.

Trick[2]: The Look Back

When working on the tagline, it is more effective to consider how you want the purchaser to feel about the product/service *after* they buy rather than when they are just contemplating a purchase. It is not only easier to come up with a tagline this way, but it will also be a much more effective statement.

Take Servpro or Apple. When one buys a MacProAir,® the message should be, and often is, *This is beautiful. I am proud of myself to have been willing to spend more money to buy the best.* When Servpro is finished cleaning up, the customer should feel relieved and surprised that their home was so well restored. It will remind the buyer that, no matter what it cost, they got the peace of mind they needed.

This is positioning via the customer's post-purchase experience. It is a *look back*.

Brand posititioning is very hard to do right; mostly it is a head game. If you see it from a satisfied customer's point of view, it is easier to take the long view. "Like it never even happened" appears riskier than "Fire & Water – Cleanup & Restoration," unless you understand the point of brand positioning, that is, to create an enduring, important bond with the customer. "A Diamond is Forever" is far more powerful than "flawless gems."

What's Next?

Now that you have your tagline and it is just as brilliant as Servpro's, it's fairly easy to backfill the tagline to be the basis for your positioning statement. The tagline provides all of the essential elements of the five rules of brand positioning.

Your brand positioning must also identify your target audience, i.e., who your customers are. Remember: if you try to include everyone (with money), you will have no focus, and no target market.

The point of differentiation is worthy of special comment. The best positions (and taglines) are generally those that *any* company in your field could have taken before you did, but because of dumb luck or lack of courage, they didn't. You got there first, so you own it – *if* you stick with it.

Everyone making tires wants to make safe tires, but no one will try to do a "Michelin" by emphasizing saftey of the family over all else. If they do, they only prove that Michelin was right and they are a wannabe.

Servpro is the same. Any cleanup company could have made the same claim. Now it's too late. Can you imagine, "XYC co. We also make you forget the disaster."

Servpro's brand position could be characterized as:

> *We provide a cleanup and restoration service; customers know that when we we are finished, their worries will be gone and they will forget what a mess it was.*

Compare that to the previous posiitioning in their first brand image:

> *Fire & Water – Cleanup & Restoration*

Which one has your attention?

Most of your competitors will not have read this chapter, so they will either skip positioning altogether or use taglines that are dull and forgettable. This is your breakout opportunity. Take it.

Takeaways for this chapter:

1. Brand posititoning is the heart and soul of a company's message to its customers.
2. Successful positioning is the most difficult challenge in brand marketing.
3. Creating a great tagline first can make that challenge easier.
4. The most critical rule of brand positioning is to connect deep in the mind of your customer.
5. Try the "look back" technique of analyzing existing customer experiences as a way to find the right words.
6. Once you have the positioning, the pressure to choose a "bad" brand (see the next chapter) is reduced, because the brand is merely the carrier of the positioning message.

Chapter 4

Broken Brands

and

The first rule of brand creation

If you have met the challenge of brand positioning, then you've overcome the greatest impediment to becoming brand-centric. Meeting the next challenge will appear easy, but don't be deceived – there is still a high risk at this point of getting seriously derailed. Chapters 4 and 5 will present incredibly simple concepts. Yet, they are the most common brand creation mistakes, so they are not as easy to avoid as they first appear.

To become a brand-centric company ultimately depends on whether you have done what is necessary to get **ownership** of your brands. Without ownership, it impossible to create brand equity, no matter how much you promote your brand. It does not matter if your brand positioning and your execution of your brand strategy are perfect. Without ownership, you still wind up with zero.

This chapter is about creating a brand which you *can* own. The next chapter is about creating a brand which you *do* own.

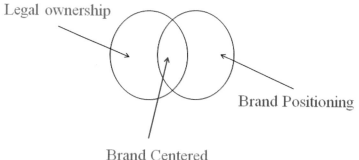

In this chapter, the discussion of brands will focus on *trademarks*. A brand and a trademark are not the same. Think of the brand as the entire Earth, which is made of several layers. At the *core* is the *trademark*, which is the *legal* right to exclusive ownership of the brand, be it a word, phrase, color, shape, etc. Surrounding the trademark is the brand positioning, the *message* of the brand. The layers beyond are your detailed story (sometimes called "messages"), which are aligned with the brand's positioning but get into the details of what you have to sell. Together, trademark, positioning, and the story are the *brand*.

Based on this model, what becomes immediately apparent is that if the *core* is somehow defective, the brand is broken, and no amount of brute force marketing is going to fix it.

The trademark is also the *core* of a business' *transferable value*, which is something that can be bought and sold. A trademark converts a non-transferable asset, (i.e. reputation), into a transferable one, (a legal trademark right). Thus, in terms of transferable value, if the trademark legal right is missing or defective, there is no transferable value.

There are two things that can cause the trademark to be defective. They form the first and second rules of brand creation.

Rule 1:

Rule 1 says that if **no one** can own it (word, phrase, color, etc.), then it isn't really a trademark and hence can never create brand equity, not for your company or any company.

Think of brand equity as being like a bucket:

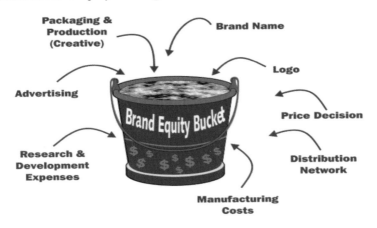

If the trademark is ownable, then when you promote the brand, the bucket fills with brand equity. But if the bucket has a hole in it, or has no bottom at all, no brand equity ever accumulates. If the word (brand) violates Rule 1, it can't accumulate brand equity. Rule 1 is about a bucket that has NO bottom. It is not a trademark

Violating Rule 1 happens when a company selects or creates a word or phrase, thinking it can be a trademark when in fact it cannot. Imagine a company developing the perfect brand strategy, perfect positioning, and powerful messaging, only to discover that the words they are using as their brand (trademark) do not qualify as a trademark at all. They own nothing. Never did. Never will. Yet this happens all of the time. Why? Because the intuitive concept of brand does not align with the legal rules of trademark. In other words, what you think is a great brand may not be a trademark at all, and since the trademark is at the core of being a brand-centric company, one cannot violate the trademark law and still have a brand.

The legal term for these words, which can never be ownable trademarks is "generic" and "merely descriptive." If it is a *generic*, or a term that *merely describes* the product or service, or an *attribute* of the product or service, then Rule 1 is violated and it is game over for the brand strategy.

The simplest example is "Beer" used for…beer products. It is a generic and can never be a trademark for beer. "Soft," for tissue, is descriptive of an *attribute* of the product, and thus also cannot be a trademark. A brand with one of these words for a trademark is a broken brand, and in most cases it cannot be fixed. If the selected word or words are either generic or merely descriptive of the product or attribute of a product, then building a brand around these words is futile.

So: Rule 1 means that if the brand merely **describes** the product or service, or even an **attribute** of the product or service, it **can't be a trademark**. If it can't be a legal trademark, a company can't own it. It's just a word in the public domain. If no one can own it, *anyone* can use if (though not as a trademark) and it can't accumulate brand equity, and it can't have transferable value. It also can't be enforced against a copyist. Everyone can use it. In other words, it is not a brand, but merely a *description*.

This rule is simple enough to understand, but it is astonishing how frequently it is ignored, to the detriment of the brand creator and his/her company.

There is actually a reason why it is often ignored: **there is a nearly *irresistible force* which drives marketers to intentionally select descriptive terms as brands.**

That irresistible force is the desire to avoid the hard work of branding, that is, the task of convincing your target audience to remember your brand and your brand positioning. Imagine if you could somehow skip that hard work of building a brand and take a *short cut*. Wouldn't you do it?

That's the problem: the workaround looks like a great time saver, but the outcome is always disaster.

If one looks at the number of broken brands in the marketplace, it is easy to see the challenge, and the need for the rule.

Let's start with the easy ones:

Example 1: The opt out

"Exceptional Value" Instant Rice. *Exceptional value* is a description of an *attribute* of the product. It is a deliberate effort NOT to brand the product. "Instant Rice" is obviously a generic term and also cannot be a trademark.

The brand message here:

Unpredictable (and presumably cheaper) –

but you have no idea of the quality of the product in the box, and that was intentional!

This non-brand also says:

> *Sometimes we buy our rice from South Carolina. Sometimes from South Korea. Rice from different places cooks and tastes different, so when you buy ours, it will be a surprise!*

The marketer clearly isn't trying to convey any sense of quality or uniformity, the hallmarks of a brand. The message here is: our product is *unpredictable*. The opposite of branding.

It seems that this store was trying to see how much bad will they could generate with customers. In that respect they succeeded.

Example 2: The *illusion* of a brand

This isn't a trick question. Is something a *house brand* if you *brand* it **HOUSE** BRAND?

Answer: Absolutely not. "House Brand" is not a trademark (or brand) even though it has the word *brand* in it. "House Brand" is a generic term, and capitalizing it won't help. One can only ask: What were they thinking? The answer is that this marketer knew little about trademark, brands, and why companies need them.

Example 3: The "I hate brands" brand

What if you *deny* that you have a brand by calling your products "No Name"? Do you have a trademark? In the words of Marissa Tomei (in *My Cousin Vinny*), *"*That is a trick question." The answer is YES. As awful of a brand as it is, NO NAME qualifies as a trademark (US registration number 1,601,126) because, unlike *Exceptional Value*, it does not: a) describe the product, or b) describe an attribute of the product.

This brand is like the "Who's on first?" joke. It is saying that our *brand* name is "NO NAME" (never mind that a product with no name is a generic...). Even though NO NAME qualifies as a legally registerable trademark, it wastes precious brand equity playing with words. The message they are trying to convey:

We hate brands. We think we are cute. Did it work?

Did you get the joke? Most people didn't – the company went under.

Example 4: Does using English generic terms in a foreign country fix a broken brand?

The first one is Danish. CAT (brand) what? Yes, cat food. Not a trademark.

The second, Soapy brand liquid soap, is from the Netherlands. "Soapy" is an attribute of the product and would not be registerable as a trademark in North America. But it is registered in the Netherlands (0846018). How can that be?

71

First, it was registered in the Netherlands as a *composite* trademark. That is, it is a combination of a three-dimensional bottle having a unique shape, and the trademark portion that includes the blue figure. The trademark covers the *combination*. It does **not** mean that they own the right to the word "Soapy" alone. Further, it is revealing that the owner did not file to register "Soapy" as a word trademark *alone.* It would have been refused registration.

The simple answer to whether foreign intrigue fixes an otherwise broken brand is *no*. If it is merely descriptive in English, then using English instead of Dutch or Danish won't fix it.

Example 5: How about the reverse—if the brand is a generic term in a foreign language, can it be a legal trademark in the US or other English-speaking country?

Is it still beer if we call it Cerveza? (Does using a foreign language transform a generic into a trademark?)

The proper trademark lawyer's answer is: sometimes, but rarely. The rule is, if the foreign word is known by a significant part of the target population to be a generic term for that population, then it can't be a trademark in the US.

If the word *beer* was translated into Navajo, **bizhéé' hólóní** (and was not specifically marketed to the Navajo market), then it would likely be considered a legal trademark because the target audience would assume it was just a *made up* word. But *cerveza*? No. Too many people know Spanish.

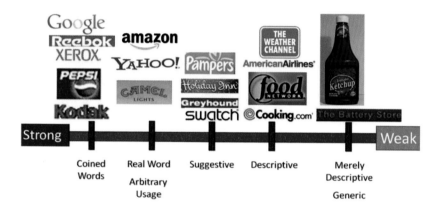

To bring clarity to all of this, the BRAND SPECTRUM provides an easy tool to measure the strength of a trademark.

The general rule is, if a word *merely describes the product* or an attribute of the product, it can't be a trademark. If it can't be a trademark, it can't be owned or enforced against others who might otherwise be infringers of the trademark. This is always true of generic terms. Beer (brand) for beer is never a trademark. For merely descriptive terms, which are not generic, there are some exceptions. The point of this book, however, it to provide best practices, not to see if you can squeeze through an exception. Some of these exceptions will be discussed, but they are not recommended.

In the main, there are trademarks of three basic strengths:

1. Very strong: of coined (made up) words or arbitrary words (real words which mean nothing with respect to the product they are used upon).
2. Weaker: called *suggestive* and the weakest, *descriptive.*
3. Broken: *merely descriptive* and *generic*, which are not trademarks at all. (Notice that the type "merely descriptive" is very different from "descriptive" in term of ownership. Both qualify as very weak, but the latter can, in some countries, be resuscitated from the near-dead.)

It's a Darwinian system. The strongest brands have a greater chance of survival. Not all strong brands do survive, but the strongest have an extra edge over weaker ones. Amongst the world's great brands, strong ones (coined and arbitrary words) are, not accidentally, more prevalent. See the Brand Spectrum chart above. The names in the coined and arbitrary categories are both famous and supremely valuable. It is absolutely no accident. Strong trademarks retain the most brand equity and are often the most valuable brands on the planet.

Every brand can be fitted on this spectrum. Try plugging in your company's brands. If some of them are merely descriptive or generic, they are in violation of Rule 1 and will never create a valuable and transferable asset. Nor can your company block others from using them. You may discover that your company has been riding a very crippled (brand) horse and you need to consider whether you want to ride that horse into the sunset. If you are thinking it won't matter, please reread Chapter 2 about transferable value. Privately held companies will discover that their brand/company name is not ownable and thus have no value, no matter how many years they have invested in building it up. Your company will be worth only its salvage value. It's a hard truth, but better to know it now rather than later.

The Difference Between *Descriptive* and Generic/*Merely Descriptive*

"Generic" and "merely descriptive" are not legally the same, but for practical purposes, you can assume they are. They are both incapable of being trademarks and thus violate Rule 1. A generic trademark would be *Sugar* as a brand for sugar while a merely descriptive one would be *Sweet*. Sweetness is an undeniable attribute of sugar and thus cannot become a trademark for sugar, and cannot be owned. (If you don't see the difference, it doesn't matter, as long as you realize such names are in brand purgatory.)

Words that *purely* describe what a product is or does can't be used as a trademark because they are an attempt to exclude the rest of the world from using or uttering those words. In short, no one can *hijack* the language for private use. Beer is generic for beer. "RED" for painter's tape is merely descriptive if the tape is red in color. It's not generic, but don't be too troubled by the difference. The point is that both are bad because no one can own them.

This is where it gets tricky.

There is this strange legal animal called a "descriptive" trademark. Note that the word "merely" is missing here. The "descriptive" trademark gets special treatment in the US, though in most foreign countries, it is still a broken brand, and of no value.

The Weather Channel is a very famous brand, but the individual words (THE, WEATHER, and CHANNEL) are entirely descriptive.

In 1982, Weather Channel, Inc. filed to register the trademark "The Weather Channel" at the US Patent and Trademark Office. The application was rejected as merely descriptive. They appealed but were rejected again. Then, years later, when The Weather Channel had become better known, they sought registration with the combination of

75

the words, plus the logo (the blue box). This time they got the registration but had to specifically agree not to claim ownership of the words "The Weather Channel" without the blue box. In other words, they only owned the combination of blue box and words, but could not make a claim to ownership for either the words or blue box separately. That was a huge concession, but necessary at the time.

By 1990, The Weather Channel's fame had increased substantially, and this time they applied to register the words "The Weather Channel" without the blue box. They got the registration, but they still had to give up the right to claim exclusive ownership of the word "weather."

They have applied for and received many more trademark registrations, but they have always had to give up exclusive rights to the word "weather." "Weather" is clearly generic for weather forecasting. If The Weather Channel were to have obtained exclusive rights to the word "weather," what would Channel 5 news call their (weather) forecast?

This is a classic example of a brand that started out millimeters from the edge of an abyss (Generic Canyon), and by a phenomenal amount of marketing (and pretty clever lawyering), has clawed its way into being a somewhat ownable brand, just *barely*. Yet, no matter how much marketing it does, it will not be allowed to own the word *weather*. That word belongs to all of us – it is generic.

There is a danger in telling this story as a *success* story. Some might conclude that there really is no problem picking a merely descriptive term and turning it into a famous and valuable brand, like The Weather Channel. But the dustbin of history is filled with many merely descriptive marks that didn't make it. Their owners achieved zero brand equity and their brand did not survive due diligence at the time of sale. More importantly, when the (costly) battle to get a descriptive brand registered was over, The Weather Channel company didn't end up owning much. What they won was very limited, and their ability to stop similar brands is likewise small. The current cable competitor to The Weather Channel is Weather Nation. The Weather Channel company can't do anything about competition using the word "weather." On the other hand, perhaps the Weather Nation company could have been more creative in its brand selection. Likewise, by using a descriptive word as their trademark, they are building a very weak brand as well.

There is a lesson in this you should be aware of, beyond the fact that bad trademarks are a bad idea. The lesson is that marketers, having perceived The Weather Channel as a successful co-opting of the term weather, will tend to follow with similarly bad ideas. If you didn't know that The Weather Channel brand strategy is problematic, then you will might be motivated to copy this risky approach, because it looks good on the surface.

In other words, making a descriptive mark tenuously ownable doesn't make it very enforceable. Relatively small changes in an (alleged) infringer's trademark may escape an infringement claim because the trademark owner has a very weak hold on the trademark.

The reason companies violate Rule 1 and choose merely descriptive marks (or, Why would anyone want to make a deal with the brand devil?)

If selecting a descriptive term is such a bad idea, why is it so commonly done?

There is an insatiable desire to use descriptors as brands because it is so much easier to *explain* to prospective customers what the product/service does if the description is built right into the name of the brand itself.

Clearly, if a person had never heard of Rule 1, they would rush to use descriptors as brands, thinking their job of marketing is made so much easier and, as a bonus, they can **lock out** their competitors from using a similar descriptive term. Of course, this kind of logic is built on an entirely false understanding of trademark law, and in the end, the law wins.

While a descriptive "brand" would *appear* to make the job of marketing easier, that is a very short term advantage. After a short time, copyists will zero in on the weakness of this trademark, and the cost of defending the mark will skyrocket. In the end, most descriptive marks are indefensible against all but exact copies. As similar marks crowd out the weak, descriptive one, the brand value of the weak descriptor gets so weak that it becomes all but worthless. So, while there is a short term advantage to a trademark that is a descriptor, there will be a perpetual hemorrhage of brand equity and fees as the company tries to defend what is likely a hopeless case.

It is always better to be smart than lucky.

But wait, didn't The Weather Channel succeed? The Weather Channel's brand choice was very risky. It has sort-of worked out for them, but it could have easily gone south, and in some respects it has (see below).

The chances of your company choosing a very weak trademark and then becoming the next The Weather Channel are not good. And why would anyone willingly subject themselves to years of costly legal defense?

There is second reason why using descriptors is not a good idea. By way of explanation, consider the story of one of the world's greatest brands, which might also have ended up in the dustbin of brand history.

How Amazon Dodged a Bullet

In 1995, Jeff Bezos had choices to make. He wildly assumed that people really don't need to *hold* a book in their hands in order to *buy* it. In fact, with so many books to look through, it might be more valuable to know what other customers thought were the best books. He reckoned that the place to start would be technical books, which were virtually impossible to find in a regular bookstore anyway. Thus there was an immediate need he could solve: to create the world's largest technical bookstore online. He also figured technical types are pretty introverted as a group and would actually prefer to shop online rather than go to the mall.

Of course he was right – about technical book buyers, but also about *all* book buyers.

Wouldn't it be great to go to a bookstore that had every book in print, a picture and a few pages of the book, and reviews by others who had actually read the books? An online bookstore had another a big advantage: in the virtual world you don't rub shoulders with actual people, only electronically connected ones. How would you feel if you were in the *Self Help* or *Sex* section of a real bookstore and some stranger came up to you to expound on his favorite titles in that section? Creepy. Yet it happens all the time on Amazon, and customers feel secure in their anonymity. Sometimes virtual exchanges are better than real ones.

In any case, the idea was brilliant. Then came the question of what to name such a company. We know, from court records from 1995, how Bezos picked the name Amazon. Obviously, he needed a trademark that also had an available dot-com domain. Assume that the following domains were available for the usual fee of $10 from Network Solutions, the domain registrar of the day:

BOOKS.COM   AMAZON.COM

Which would you have chosen? No cheating. It was 1995. Selling books online was a fool's pipe dream.

According to The Weather Channel school of branding, it seems like a complete no-brainer. Ten bucks for Books.com!? Grab it.

Common reasoning:

> Go with the name that instantly tells what it is, for Pete's sake!
>
> Calling it something strange, like Google, Yahoo, or even Twitter, means it will take time for the customer to figure out what's being sold under the brand. Who's got time for that?
>
> Furthermore, with Books.com, no one else can call their company Books dot anything. Right?

Of course, this reasoning is entirely wrong.

Brand expert reasoning:

Common sense is fine, but the rules of branding are a mix of law and art and not intuitive. Taking the quick and dirty route (descriptive brands) is a non-stop flight to brand purgatory.

As has been shown, Books.com would be a poor choice. "Books" will always be as generic as "weather," and no one would be able to stop Books.edu, Books.tv, or even Books.xxx. That last one might really do some damage to your reputation.

In prior chapters it was demonstrated that brands are strong when they are aligned with a clear message, their brand position. Remember Apple's brand message:

> *It shall always be beautiful and easy to use*

Amazon's initial position was something along the lines of:

> *Finding the right book can be a daunting task. We have a community of fellow readers who can help you based on their experiences.*

When selecting a descriptive term like Books.com, what is lost is the flexibility to infuse a *specific* brand message in the trademark. The word "books" is so descriptive that the reader has already made up their mind about what is sold under the brand, *leaving little opportunity to explain the brand's true story*. In other words, selecting descriptors also seriously limits the opportunity to tell your point of differentiation. The descriptive term is too strong.

For example, if the brand is Plywood Minnesota, and the unique feature of the store is no longer selling plywood, and is no longer in Minnesota, then how does one get past the fact that those two descriptive terms are built right into the brand? If you select a brand with a product attribute in the brand name, you are forever stuck with that attribute.

Ok, how did Bezos land on "Amazon"?

There are many stories, but the most viable is this one. His first choice was **Cadabra.com**, but he worried that it sounded too much like "cadaver." He went with the letter A because Yahoo, the search engine of the day, always listed search results in alphabetical order. (By the way, Cadabra.com is currently for sale, if anyone is interested.)

No matter. You know the rest of the story. Bezos plunks down the $10, gets the Amazon domain and builds one of the world's greatest companies, which sells books.

Of course, we all know that the choice of Amazon instead of Books.com was also brilliant for the reason that Books.com would no longer fit the scope of the products offered by Amazon. How many companies think about such outcomes when they select descriptive names?

It is no accident that most of the greatest brands in the world have super strong names: Google, Yahoo, Twitter, Kodak, Coke, Pepsi, and so on. Of course, there are some slipups, like Facebook, but Mark Zuckerberg wasn't trying to build a business when he named the website. He was looking for women to date.

In that regard, it is worth revisiting The Weather Channel brand story. Clearly this descriptive name was chosen to make sure that people reading the TV guide knew what was playing on that particular channel. Even Homer Simpson would have no trouble guessing what would be on The Weather Channel.

But wait, look at the program lineup on The Weather Channel these days. As a TV cable channel, The Weather Channel now fills less than half of its airtime with weather forecasts. It's now knee deep in reality shows like Prospectors, Ice Road Truckers, Fat Guys in the Woods, and (a personal favorite) Highway Through Hell.

Direct TV, a satellite broadcaster carrying The Weather Channel, was so upset about the channel's programming that in 2014 they dropped

The Weather Channel, claiming that it was looking too much like the Discovery Channel. The Weather Channel's reality shows are only *tangentially* related to weather, in the same way as the BBC channel considers Star Trek a British show because Patrick Stewart is a Brit. The Weather Channel's choice of a descriptive brand has boxed them in in the same way Books.com would have limited the company that became Amazon.

The pressure on The Weather Channel by the cable carriers didn't lighten up, and in September 2015, The Weather Channel agreed to get back to its core business, giving weather forecasts and getting out of reality TV shows. The problem is that The Weather Channel does not have a lock on cable weather forecasting, and the cable companies would happily drop them for a cheaper alternative (except for Comcast, which owns The Weather Channel). Furthermore, the Internet and mobile apps, including The Weather Channel app, have rendered the need for a TV channel somewhat superfluous.

The brand decision made 20 years ago is coming home to roost. In June 2015, Comcast lowered its book value on The Weather Channel by $86 million.

The Weather Channel is struggling with an identity crisis created by an early branding decision that seemed perfect at the time, but turned out to be a time bomb. Bezos' decision, whether by brilliance or dumb luck, side-stepped this whole mess.

The Weather Channel, like Amazon, needs to bust out of its confined brand, but unlike Amazon, The Weather Channel is saddled with a brand that can't adapt.

It wouldn't be surprising if The Weather Channel changes its name. The obvious choice would be TWC, but oops, that stands for Time Warner Cable.

Kentucky Fried Chicken quietly became KFC in order to get that nasty word, "fried," out of its brand. Did you notice it when it happened?

Knowing the dangers of descriptive brands, and the utter futility of trying to use a generic as a brand, it is still amazing that some marketers have not gotten the news flash: it won't work. And when someone like The Weather Channel squeaks through, it doesn't necessarily end well.

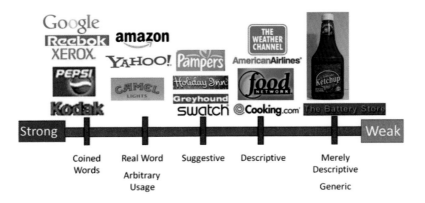

The Two Types of Super-Strong Trademarks

Strong trademarks can hold unlimited brand equity and consequently become extraordinarily valuable.

Strong brand type 1: made up (coined) words.

Each of these brands is a collection of letters that means nothing at all. They are the perfect "brand clay": they give total flexibility with brand positioning, and whatever is added to the brand offerings will "stick."

Kodak is a company in trouble, but for over 120 years it was the poster child of what a strong brand looks like. It was a casualty of a disruptive technology, and unlike Dolby, it made the wrong move into printers and cameras.

The story behind the name Kodak is as instructive as it is legendary, so it is worth retelling. George Eastman, the founder of Kodak, did not invent film, but he did revolutionize photography. Before Kodak, film was on flat glass sheets, the kind Mathew Brady used in his Civil War photography. What Eastman did was put "film" on flexible celluloid plastic and then on a spool so that cameras could take multiple pictures without changing film plates. At the same time, the light sensitivity of film was improved, making it possible to make cameras smaller. Eastman's roll film made it possible to carry a camera like the Brownie, which had the ability to take 12 pictures instead of one. He made amateur photography possible by making roll film.

If Eastman had wanted a descriptive brand name, he could have called his new company RollCo, RollOFilm, or Multishot. If he had done so, he would have boxed himself in because, ultimately, Kodak's biggest money maker was movie film and medical (x-ray) films.

Instead, the legend is that Eastman said, "I like the letter K. It shall begin and end with a K and I don't much care what is in between."

It wasn't really dumb luck that he picked a very strong brand name. He recognized that K was a letter that, unlike C, had only one pronunciation. He liked its strong sound, and at the time there were very few brands using K. He wasn't trained as a brand specialist, but he knew some of the rules.

The OREO brand also warrants further explanation. The Oreo is by far the world's best-selling cookie (though it undoubtedly is not the world's best-tasting). For that matter, McDonald's is the world's largest fast food purveyor but never claims to have great food. Apparently, best-selling beats best-tasting, at least some of the time.

"Oreo" is clearly a made up (coined) word, so it qualifies as a super-strong trademark. Many have speculated on how Nabisco came up with the name. Since nobody actually knew, a few years ago Nabisco made a very entertaining commercial telling the story, though it is completely false.

You can watch it here (http://watchworthy.com/oreo-got-name/) or do a Google® search on "how Oreo got its name."

In the video, the executives of the company are trying to pick a name for the newly created cookie. The suggestions – Waferiscious, Twisto Cookie, and Chockorama – are offered up. The executives then turn to a meek employee in the shadows, Hurley, who responds with a muffled, "I dunno," which they hear as *Oreo*. Genius, they exclaim! And so it is.

But could it have happened that way?

The beauty of this story is that Waferiscious, Twisto Cookie, or Chockorama would have been the name most companies would prefer, and Hurley's idea could have gotten him fired.

Would you have had the courage to call the cookie Oreo? Would you have had the *courage* to name your company Google or Twitter? Or a chocolate drop in the shape of a plumb-bob, Kisses?

If your company understood the power of a brand and the freedom a coined name creates, perhaps.

Strong brand type 2: words that mean *something*, but *not with respect to the product or service* to which they are associated.

HUH?

They are real words, but not descriptive. "Target" would be descriptive for *archery* targets, but not for big box retail stores.

The brands shown above are among the world's most valuable. Here are some more within the top 100: Google, Apple, IBM, Microsoft, McDonald's, Coca-Cola, Visa, AT&T, Marlborough, Amazon, Verizon, GE, Facebook, Wal-Mart, Disney, American Express, Samsung, LV, Starbucks, BMW, Home Depot, IKEA, Siemens, FedEx, Gucci, US Bank, Yahoo, Twitter, Ford, Prada, PayPal , Pepsi, KFC.

The overwhelming majority are super strong arbitrary words which do not describe any aspect of the product. The ones in RED are the outliers and fall into the *suggestive* category on the Brand Spectrum.

One, in BLUE, used to be descriptive, but the company fixed it. KFC, previously Kentucky Fried Chicken, realized that the word *fried* spelled *t-r-o-u-b-l-e* and dropped all of the words from their name. The right honorable Colonel Sander's image remains as is, the second trademark.

The Compromise: Suggestive Trademarks

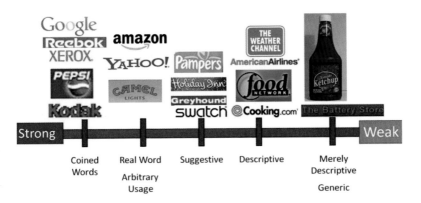

While generic/merely descriptive words can never become trademarks, and descriptive words are a roll of the dice with the devil, there is a class of trademark that is much weaker than coined words but still qualifies as ownable.

This class of trademarks is *suggestive* of the product or service it refers to, but less than descriptive. This class is really a spectrum of its own, spanning from *very* suggestive to *slightly* suggestive. Of course, the less suggestive, the stronger the mark.

All of the above marks are suggestive, but they too span the spectrum. For example, WRANGLER is mildly suggestive, so it is almost equivalent to an arbitrary word, which is the strongest kind of mark.

Dove, Ivory, Suave, and Coppertone are definitely suggestive of an attribute of the product so are somewhere in the middle of the suggestive spectrum. A Roach Motel is never going to be a *motel*, even if roaches could read the sign, so it is only suggestive. Chick-fil-A and Sweettarts are suggestive, tending toward descriptive. Spray 'n Wash is mighty close to the wrong side of the boundary between suggestive and descriptive.

Branding Tricks (which won't work)

Now that the trademark system is understood, one may be tempted to *game the system*. To spare you the trouble of a lengthy litigation to find out whether your brand will work, here are some ways marketers have tried (and failed) to make descriptive marks seem not so descriptive:

1. Use a *corrupted* spelling of a generic term to make it a real trademark.
    a. Example: Kleen (for cleaning supplies)
    b. General rule: All spellings, including misspellings, count as if they were spelled correctly. Corrupted spellings never work.
2. Use a foreign word to replace English so that the term is not descriptive.
    a. Example: Cerveza (Spanish for beer)
    b. General rule: If the language is generally known to a significant (not majority) of the target public, the foreign word is considered

synonymous with English and thus still generic. BUT it doesn't take much to make this one work. If the foreign word itself is nonstandard, there is a much better chance of its having value as a brand. LEGO is slang Danish for Le' Go', pronounced in Danish Lay go', meaning "play well." VOLVO is Latin for "I roll" or "to roll." Latin is not a spoken language; a few in the target audience might know the root of the verb (volver), but an abstract Latin term is unlikely to be recognized by the average English speaker. The word is not generic.

3. Add color or stylization to a generic word to make it non-generic.

a. Example: BOOZE CRUISE
    for travel by boat to consume liquor (and avoid pesky liquor laws).
b. General rule: Genericness is analyzed on the basis of the *entire* mark in use. Here the bottle integrated into the letter B is capable of being recognized as a trademark, so it may be possible to register this mark; however, the Trademark Office is going to do their duty and protect the language. They will not likely grant the owner enforceable rights to the words booze + cruise, but only to the graphic with the special B. In terms of building a valuable brand, this doesn't cut it.

4. Add another generic/merely descriptive word to the generic term. The rule: generic + merely descriptive = no trademark.

Examples (water products):

Glaceau Smart Water is a Coca-Cola brand. It is actually a good trademark. It is registerable because "Glaceau" is a coined word and means nothing in any language. It sounds like *glacier,* but it isn't, so it's not generic. Also, "smart" clearly doesn't describe the product or any attribute of water (or, perhaps, even the people who buy it). If *smart* was part of a brand for computer chips, then *smart* might be descriptive.

Takeaways for this chapter:

1. Rule 1: *Ownership* of a brand is fundamental. If you can't own it because it is generic/merely descriptive, you will never create brand equity, and you will spend a lot of time with lawyers trying to defend your brand.
2. There is a natural impulse to violate Rule 1 because it is so easy to launch a brand if it is descriptive.
3. Most descriptive brands fail. Others hem in their owners (e.g., Books.com).
4. You might get lucky choosing a descriptive brand and making it work, but, as always, luck is not a strategy.
5. Choose stronger brands. If you want more risk, go to a casino or play in the stock market. Don't mess with your company's future.

Chapter 5

The Second Rule of Brand Creation

In the last chapter, we discussed the first rule of brand creation, which is that a company needs to select a brand that is capable of actually being a brand, so that it retains brand equity and has transferable value. Otherwise, the brand will have little or no value. If it can't be owned, it can't be sold or defended against copyists. A brand like this is a very bad choice.

Nevertheless, Rule 1 is routinely violated. Companies usually find this out at one of two critical moments: 1) when someone infringes on their "brand" and they want to stop the infringer, or 2) when the company is for sale and during due diligence it is discovered that there is no "brand" to sell, i.e., no *transferable value*.

In this chapter, we'll discuss the second rule of brand creation:

Rule 2 says that even if your brand meets Rule 1 (i.e., it is not generic or merely descriptive), but *your company does not own it*, then it can't do your company any good. Rule 1 is broken often; Rule 2 is broken even more often. Furthermore, proof that they have overlooked Rule 2 usually comes as a nasty surprise to most business owners because it arrives either in the form of a cease and desist letter from someone who *does* own the trademark, or it surfaces during the due diligence phase of a business sale.

Owning a trademark is not the same as *thinking* you own the trademark.

On the surface, this seems so completely obvious that it shouldn't even be necessary to mention it, yet Rule 2 is so commonly violated, it apparently needs much more attention.

In the world of tangible property, the concept of ownership is pretty straightforward. It is obvious that acquiring an asset without proper title is dangerous. In a real estate transaction, there is even an elaborate closing event during which the title is scrutinized before money changes hands.

Consider the scenario of purchasing a used car from a private party. After viewing the car and taking a test drive, one usually asks first about the price: "How much do you want for it?" However, the first question really should be: **"Do you own it?"** If the party doesn't own it, it won't do any good to know the price.

This question is not asked with used cars because it is *assumed* that the selling party is also the owner, and in any event, the title certificate will be proof of ownership. Yet intellectual property, an invisible asset, has no title certificate, and obtaining ownership is not so simple. There is nothing like a certificate of title for intellectual property. Worse yet, there isn't even a single consolidated place to search for clear title.

Before explaining how to avoid running afoul of Rule 2, it will be helpful to illustrate how serious a threat it is to violate the rule of ownership.

Breaking Rule 2: The Case of Amazon

In the last chapter, it became clear that Jeff Bezos's selection of the name *Amazon.com* was a stroke of genius, but there is a darker side to this story.

Bezos' company fully complied with Rule 1, picking a strong name that one can own. Bezos probably didn't know it at the time, but his company failed on Rule 2. There was a potential problem with title to the Amazon trademark, and it wasn't discovered until years after Amazon had massive brand equity in the name. It was serious enough that Amazon was at risk of not being allowed to use the Amazon brand in some, if not all, US markets.

How could this possibly happen to a company as smart and rich as Amazon? And if it can happen to Amazon, can it happen to any company? The answer is clearly: YES, unless great care is taken, in advance, to avoid this nasty surprise.

For a good 25 years, *Amazon Bookstore* quietly did business in downtown Minneapolis. This little bookstore opened in 1970 and sold books on feminist topics nationwide, by mail order, well before the existence of the Internet. They had a mailing list of 2100 regular subscribers. They later added a website.

Amazon.com started in 1995, twenty five years after Amazon Bookstore. Bezos picked the name *Amazon* because it started with an A and was the name of a great river. What is not known is how extensively (or even if) Amazon.com searched for prior users of the word *Amazon*. All we know is that they forged ahead with the brand choice in 1995.

In trademark law, it doesn't matter if a business innocently takes another company's trademark. Infringement is infringement, and while intentionally infringing (i.e., with knowledge of the prior user) is worse, "I didn't know" is not a viable defense.

In 1998, Amazon Bookstore (**AB**) started getting requests for books that they did not carry. These requests were from customers of Amazon.com. Apparently some Amazon.com customers found the name Amazon Bookstore in the phone book and decided to phone in their orders. Perhaps they thought Amazon.com had a brick and mortar store after all.

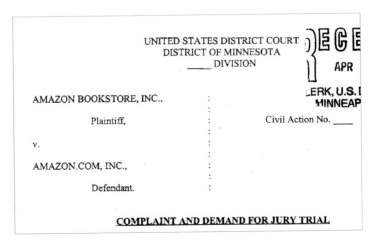

> As for the name, Bezos originally went with Cadabra Inc. (as in abracadabra) but realized that name was problematic when associates mistook it for Cadaver Inc. A three-month search for the right brand focused on words that begin with "A" so that the name would appear near the top of the alphabetized lists that were still importance in navigating the Internet. He figured the name had to be short, easy to spell, memorable and able to convey great size. Amazon Bookstore, signifying Earth's biggest river, met the bill for a company that would be Earth's biggest bookstore, without unduly constricting its flexibility. 'A lot of very deliberate thinking went into the name.' Bezos said.

In 1999, AB sued Amazon.com for trademark infringement and unfair competition in federal district court in Minnesota, where AB was located.

The battle was definitely a David vs. Goliath in terms of legal resources. AB even sold T-shirts to finance the legal battle, but they were severely financially outgunned. Still, in terms of trademark law, their case was clearly strong enough to put A.com at serious risk.

Under US trademark law, the **first user** is entitled to the trademark **registration**, unless that registration has become incontestable, which it had not (more on this later). Furthermore, and critical to Amazon.com, the first user in a particular geographic region is entitled to *exclusive* use of that trademark in that region. Looking at AB's business, they had clear prior use in Minneapolis-St. Paul and the surrounding area. Based on AB's mail order business, they had a decent argument for the prior rights in many major cities around the US.

From Amazon.com's point of view, as an Internet seller, the holes in their selling territory would be an impossible problem, especially if AB could establish prior use in the top 20 US markets. If Amazon.com was enjoined from selling in the top US markets, or even just in Minneapolis-St. Paul, how could Amazon.com run a national Internet business? There was no way to block access to Amazon.com's web site in certain zip codes, and it would be embarrassing to refuse to ship to those areas.

In the world of Internet sales, a Swiss-cheese market would have been impossible, so a lot was at stake.

In a trademark infringement case, the two key defenses are: 1) the marks are different or 2) the businesses are in different channels of trade.

As to defense 1, Amazon.com was on very shaky ground. Since the ".com" suffix of their brand is generic, it provided little to distinguish the one Amazon from the other. This meant that the trademark battle was Amazon vs. Amazon, and defense 1 (the marks are different) was likely a loser. Furthermore, Amazon is a very strong trademark for the field of books. It fits on the Brand Spectrum at Real Word – Arbitrary Usage.

Defense 2 (different channels of trade) was also very difficult to argue. Both companies sold books, so there was clear overlap.

This is where the case turned ugly, as reported in the press.

AB's books were pretty much limited to feminist topics. Amazon.com carried those books, too, but it was only a subset of their selection. Amazon.com argued that, in effect, a feminist bookstore was not a *bookstore* in the sense of Amazon.com because of its limited subject matter. (If it wasn't a bookstore, what was it? If this argument is not holding water in your mind, it's a good bet it wasn't going to fly in court either.) It was a pretty desperate and dangerous argument that hit the press (see http://www.salon.com/1999/10/28/amazon_3/). To Amazon.com's great credit, when the strategy was heard higher up within Amazon.com, they disavowed the argument that feminist bookstores are not bookstores, and some lawyers for Amazon.com lost their jobs. Shortly after, the case was settled with Amazon.com buying AB's trademark rights and granting back a short license to AB for an undisclosed amount of money. Amazon.com never admitted infringement. The case just went away, so we don't know for sure how it would have turned out; however, it is safe to say that if AB had had the resources to fight on, Amazon.com would have been in grave danger of having to change its name.

Happy ending? Yes, for Amazon.com. They had sufficient money to buy an opponent's trademark *and* their opponent was *willing* to sell. AB was not *required* to sell, but they couldn't afford to maintain the legal battle.

Would it be a happy ending for your company if it violated Rule 2 and found itself in trouble? Don't count on it. Remember, not all trademark battles involve opponents so unequal in financial strength, and not all opponents are willing to *sell* their trademarks. If the brand is the core asset of a company, the company may not even be able to *settle* without extreme damage to the company. So, if you are considering ignoring Rule 2, you may find yourself with a business without a brand. The lesson is: be prepared. **It is always better to avoid a problem in the first place than to hope to fix it later.**

Of course, the very worst time to find out you have violated Rule 2 is during due diligence in a sale of your brand. Imagine that at 11:59 pm in a due diligence to purchase a company, it's discovered: your company doesn't own its brand. This is not at all uncommon. The buyer usually walks, but if not, the seller takes a huge haircut. All of this is avoidable.

Why did Amazon.com's near train wreck happen at all?

Even in 1995, as a startup, Bezos had the help of competent trademark counsel. The case settled before it was determined why Amazon.com missed the existence of Amazon Bookstore. Since Amazon Bookstore (AB) never registered their mark, their trademark was harder to find, but hardly impossible. If Amazon.com had come across AB in a trademark clearance search, reasonably, they might have picked a different river. Nile? Mississippi? Danube?

The Importance of the Trademark Search

It might be useful to create a Rule 2.1: Just because your company has not received a cease and desist letter does not mean you have clear title. Most likely you won't find out until years later, and then you may find out that years' worth of accumulated brand equity have vanished in an instant. Imagine that Amazon.com was sued not in 1999, but in 1997, just before Amazon's IPO. The impact on stock price would have been devastating. Who would gamble on a company that might be enjoined from using its company and domain names? Sure, they could change their name to Quark.com, but at what cost in dollars and reputation?

Coca-Cola encountered this problem while planning the launch of its ill-fated SURGE soft drink. In 1997, Coca-Cola planned to launch SURGE with a Super Bowl commercial.

Something obviously went wrong in their trademark clearance search. Days before the big game, a company claiming prior rights from 1925 for a Surge-branded drink, objected to Coke's use. Then, to make matters worse, another company, which made a Surge milking machine, filed in court to enjoin the TV spot from playing, potentially leaving 30 seconds of dead air in its place and a $50 million launch meltdown for Coke. The milking machine claimant had a pretty feeble claim (perhaps not so true for the Surge drink claimant), but because of the launch date time pressure, Coke settled by paying the claimants. Still, it was a close call. As a footnote, Surge didn't make it and went dark for 10+ years, but is back in a test re-launch, only available by mail order through…Amazon.

This sort of trouble doesn't usually show up at launch, but rather, when a product is already successful, claimants come out of the woodwork. In more practical terms, ***can a company afford to change the name of a product or service several years after its launch***?

The Dreaded Due Diligence

The second opportunity for trouble, as mentioned, is when *selling* the company. Any buyer's attorney worth his/her salt will find a title fault in the trademark, if one exists, and advise the buyer that the purchase price needs to be re-evaluated with the value of the brand equity zeroed out, or at least reduced. Violating Rule 2 can be very expensive.

Yet this is all largely preventable.

To understand how to avoid the problem of a surprise brand meltdown, it's important to understand how one can get clear title to a brand.

Trademark Rights Pyramid

In the United States, there is a three-tier trademark system. Think of each tier as a challenge to be met to get clear title to a trademark.

The king of trademark title: Federal trademark registration

At the top of the pyramid is the US federal trademark registration system. Federal trademark registrations are not all-powerful, but they are as good as it gets in terms of national brand ownership.

The United States Patent and Trademark Office (USPTO) receives trademark applications for registration. It conducts a search and examination of each application, and if they meet legal requirements, they will be granted as trademark registrations on the Principal Trademark Register (which will be referred to as simply "federal trademark registrations").

The search and examination process checks to see if the proposed trademark meets the following:

1. The mark is really *capable* of being a trademark. (Remember Rule 1: if it is generic or merely descriptive, it can't be owned. The Trademark Office will reject such applications.)
2. The mark is not "confusingly similar" to another registered or pending trademark in the federal database. (Rule 2)
3. The mark is not prohibited from registration for other reasons (e.g., the mark is immoral, scandalous, or violates some special rules, such as the one prohibiting the use of names of former Presidents).

If the mark gets through the examination process, it is published for third parties to object to the Trademark Office's decision to issue the trademark. That third-party process is called an Opposition, which creates a small 30-day challenge period.

Granted federal registrations have very powerful rights, primarily because they give a company the coveted *transferable value*. The most important is national trademark rights, subject to any pre-existing unregistered user who used the mark before the filing date of the application. See Common Law right below and beware!

The second most valuable right is that the registration holder can be granted *incontestability* status after five years of registration. Incontestability means that the trademark can never be cancelled by a claimant with prior trademark use rights. This is the gold standard for a brand.

The zombie marks:

The federal examination database does not search for prior users who have not filed for *federal* registration. These are the dreaded common law users. Common law trademark users are a bit like **zombies**: they show up unexpectedly, they are hard to get rid of, and they can ruin your day (and brand). Remember Surge?

Even if you get a federal registration, a common law user has the right to continue using the same trademark in a limited geographic area where they had been using the mark *before the filing date* of your federal trademark.

What is critical in a trademark clearance search is that your trademark attorney finds and evaluates the risks posed by all common law users. Make certain that the attorney you retain has deep experience in detecting these potential hazards and protects you early in the process. This is challenging even for seasoned trademark attorneys, and likely complex to marketers.

State registration

Next on the Trademark Rights Pyramid are the trademark registration systems of each of the 50 states and some of the US territories. For practical purposes, state trademark registrations are just classy common law users. The difference is that there is a specific place to search the state trademark offices, so prior users having state registrations are fairly easy to find.

Warning: state registrations are NOT the same as corporate name registrations, which every Secretary of State's office maintains. This means that registering a company with the Secretary of State absolutely does NOT grant the right to use the name as a trademark. *This is a huge trap.* Most privately held companies are incorporated and assume their trademark/brand rights in the company name are secure. Nothing could be further from the truth.

The Secretaries of State of nearly all states will grant a corporate registration (which is not a trademark) to any corporation with a name that is not *identical* to an existing one. They don't have the time, expertise, or inclination to figure out which are infringing. That is the company's problem. Most companies – and many corporate lawyers – don't realize this.

Each state will also grant state trademark registrations. Most states will also grant registrations to marks that are similar but not identical. Thus, states routinely grant trademarks that infringe on other trademarks in their state. Not their problem. Furthermore, no state checks their trademark filings against other states. Again, states leave it to the companies to monitor state trademark registrations and to act if an infringer tries to register.

As previously mentioned, at the bottom tier of the US trademark system are "common law" rights. This term, "common law," is frequently used in relation to marriage. In a very few states, if two people live together long enough and act like they are married, the state may consider them married without the formality of a marriage license. While common law marriage is disappearing, common law trademark is not.

If one uses a trademark, one automatically gains *limited* trademark rights without the formality of filing for registration. This right, however, is strictly limited to the geographical area where it is actively in use.

The purpose of common law rights is to protect careless companies who fail to file for federal or state registration. It is a very poor way to protect trademark rights, but it is better than nothing, as Amazon Bookstore (AB) found out. Most other countries do not grant common law trademark rights: either you have a registration, or you have nothing.

The problem with common law rights, from the point of view of a company trying to get clear title to a trademark, is that earlier common law users pose a permanent threat to a later user, and there is **no organized way to find them**. Because they are not registered anywhere, there is no single place to search for them. They might be in a phone book, on a web page, or merely have a storefront with a name on the building. Or, they might be an obscure mail order company that is virtually invisible to any kind of search.

Thus, a comprehensive trademark search involves turning over every leaf in as many places as possible. There are database companies that can provide the raw data for a search, but the real issue is how to *interpret* the results. A professional database search will often produce megabytes of potential matches, many of which will be false positives. Of course the trick is knowing which are false. It is essential to find a highly experienced (10+ years) legal specialist, who regularly works in trademark search analysis, to know how to read and interpret the results.

The problem Amazon.com and Coke/Surge faced was that either 1) their search was inadequate, 2) they didn't search at all, or 3) they *did* find the prior common law users, but got too self-assured that a common law user would never object.

While we can't know what happened in these two cases, it is pretty clear that the costs/ benefits of doing a very thorough trademark clearance search are worth their weight in gold, a lot of gold. The typical cost/leverage ratio for finding a trademark title problem in advance is at least 10,000 to 1. That means for every dollar spent in title clearance, the cost of fixing/litigating/buying out a title problem is 10,000x. Sometimes these title problems can be fatal to a brand and/or company.

Anecdotal analysis of a number of randomly chosen, *privately held* companies produced surprising results: when asked, 100% of companies believed they owned their brand. On further inspection, the number was about two thirds of these companies did *not* own their company name. Most probably could never even get clear title to it if they tried. None of them knew about this time bomb. Most often they thought they owned their company name because they had either a Secretary of State corporate registration for that name, or they owned the *Internet domain*. Sadly, both of these assumptions are dead wrong. Domain names are *subservient* to the owner of the registered trademark and, as mentioned, Secretary of State registrations are substantially meaningless. As these owners look to sell their company, or license their brand, in a due diligence search it will be discovered that they have no brand equity, and they (or their buyer) could face an infringement suit.

Speaking from experience, it's a safe bet that companies operating with the mistaken belief that they own their brands are oblivious to the fact that they have a problem. They are also the ones who stand to lose the most by not fixing the problem. Imagine—you have used a company name/brand that you don't actually own for 20+ years unaware of the ownership issue. Is ignorance really bliss? Tick, tick tick...

By the way, you may be wondering why the federal trademark system has such a big flaw that grants those zombie common law trademark owners such powerful rights. No other country gives these zombies such power. It is not actually a flaw; rather, it was done by intentional design. Like Amazon Bookstore (AB), there are companies who fail to take advantage of the federal or state trademark systems, mostly by ignorance. The US trademark system still gives them limited geographic rights by mere use, without registration. Almost all other countries have eliminated common law trademarks because of the mess they create.

Waking up Sleeping Dogs

There are three common ways for a dormant brand title/ownership problem to appear.

The first is **expansion**. Expanding the use of the brand, typically by enlarging geography, i.e., using the brand in a new territory, is an easy was to stir up trouble. A hair salon in Los Angles may expand to San Diego, which triggers an illegal expansion of common law rights. If someone has a trademark registration for the same trademark in the same field, a competitor cannot expand their geographic extent. They are locked out of further expansion by the trademark registrant.

The second way to get into trouble is to use the same brand on a **broader range** of goods/services. For example, a company uses "Quark" for insurance products, but never registers. They later decide to use Quark on financial services That is an expansion into a different "channel of trade" and may trigger an infringement.

Even if these first two trigger events (enlarging geography and broadening scope of use) don't occur, the third one will almost always show up: **due diligence**.

When a business is being sold, there will be a thorough due diligence process of the buyer looking for skeletons in the closet. Brand/trademark title will most certainly be investigated.

Not long ago, a client needed assistance in purchasing software code for a project. The price was $1 million. The client asked that the transaction be done with a minimum of paperwork. Normally in such a transaction, the seller is required to warrant that certain things in the sale are true. Such things include whether the financial statements are accurate, whether there are lawsuits or threats, and so on. In this transaction, the client authorized that ONE question could be put to the buyer. Faced with the dilemma of protecting a client in this transaction, what single question would be the absolute most important question to ask the seller? Does the software work? Were there any known bugs? Had it ever been hacked? Is there good documentation of the source code?

Those are good questions, but entirely irrelevant to the mother of all questions a buyer should ask, which by now you know is: **Do you own it?**

No other question matters without the right answer to this one. In the case of my client, the seller's answer was a shocking: *We don't know.*

The reason they didn't know was that they had acquired the software from a prior company, who had employed numerous subcontractors. Because they had never gotten the necessary title documents from any of the prior owners, at the end of the day, they didn't have clear title and they had no way to get it. The real answer to that single question was not "I don't know," it was, NO – we don't own it. The deal fell through on that one question. Did the software have bugs? Did it work? It really didn't matter.

Any company considering a future sale must know if it owns (i.e., has clear title to) its brand name. Looking at the business from the *buyer's* perspective, most buyers hope to leverage the brand to make the business even more profitable. That might mean developing new products and/or geographic expansion. When a brand gets new exposure, it takes on new risks. During the due diligence process, the buyer needs to find out what surprises await them. Even though "sleeping dogs" may have been quiet for decades, the buyer can't count on those dogs continuing to slumber. Furthermore, the buyer is likely to want to grow the business in ways which *directly trigger* those dogs into action. That is due diligence. Thus a buyer is **more** concerned about the quality of the trademark rights (i.e., Rule 2) than even the seller.

Similarly, when launching a product/service, there won't be any trademark infringement issues until the product is *peaking* in value. The attention success creates will also inspire prior trademark rights holders to act. There is never a good time to receive a cease and desist letter, but post-launch is the worst. Ask Coke.

Recovery or *Avoidance*: **Which is Cheaper?**

Almost all brands have some sort of prior rights problem. It is critical to find out how serious the problem is before someone else finds it, either in due diligence or by a cease and desist letter. Prior rights problems can be discovered by doing a very thorough professional trademark clearance search.

Having experience with thousands of trademark clearance searches, the best advice is: don't skimp on this one. The advice of Red Adair is dead on:

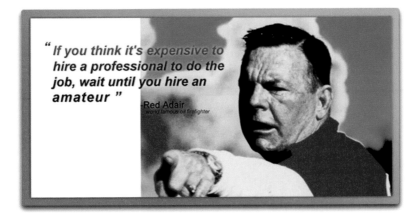

Don't make this mistake yourself. The cost of a mistake is 10,000x the cost of doing it right the first time. What would it cost to defend a trademark infringement lawsuit? $500k-$1.5M. What would it cost to rebrand a company/product/service after building brand equity for five or more years? Even if you have the benefit of access to specialized databases, only an experienced professional will have the knowledge to know how to analyze the data and detect the nuances. There are a great many amateurs out there willing to do this work. But fixing their errors due to naïveté or inexperience is always expensive. The motto, *you don't know what you don't know,* really applies to trademark clearance.

For those who cannot resist the DIY method, realize that the available data will almost certainly lead to false positives *and* false negatives. This will likely result in discarding a good mark or keeping a bad one, both for the wrong reasons. The USPTO (Trademark Office) online database is not adequate, and the search tools are very primitive. One can use the Internet to look for problem trademarks, but it is hazardous to analyze the results without the help of an expert who is well versed in search analyses. The Internet is not an adequate database and does not provide key analytical data, such as date of first use, other registrations, litigiousness, etc.

Unless your company has an unlimited amount of money to spend on trademark clearance, it makes sense to be smart about the selection of candidate names. The reality is that on the Brand Spectrum, the names that have the least chance of clearing a search are *suggestive* marks. It's purely mathematical. Most marketers gravitate to suggestive names (after descriptives) because they are perceived as "helpful" to brand understanding. Even though that perception is ultimately damaging to the brand, there is a lot of activity in suggestive names. Hence most of them are taken.

The following technique is helpful in dealing with the psychological forces that drive people to bad/unavailable brand choices.

First, I have the client create a list of five prospective trademarks for each of these trademark types:

1. Suggestive (which are easiest to come up with). For example: "Pampers."
2. Coined words (which are harder to generate). For example: "Google."
3. Real words, but unrelated to the product (which are hardest). For example: "Amazon."

Without this requirement, *all* marks you create will end up falling into the suggestive category, and few if any will clear the search. Notice that there is no suggestion to make a list of descriptive words. These are losers, and the odds of winning the lottery, as The Weather Channel did, are just too low.

111

After you've generated your list, *for each trademark type*, rank the five names you've come up with.

The next step is to conduct a preliminary screening search on the top contenders from <u>each type</u>. Screening is at the federal level only. By experience, this is only about 60% accurate, but it is sufficient to cull out the easily unavailable names and is much less expensive than a full clearance search. In reality, it is the suggestive marks that usually fail to make the cut.

The client then re-evaluates the results. If there are no survivors (or not enough), additional candidates get a pre-screen; otherwise, on to the comprehensive search.

A comprehensive search is conducted for the client's top candidate. This means searching the federal database again, but this time with a high-powered algorithm that can pick up more sound-alikes and other tricky marks. For example, in searching for "snuggle," would one find "cuddle"?

The next part of the analysis is a combination of art and science. In the US, this entails a sophisticated search of the federal trademark register, the 50 state trademark registers, and then the mother of all searches, the common law. Usually, search results are 500+ pages and most are common law, unregistered usages. Of the citations found that are tangentially relevant, even deeper searches must be conducted to determine for which products/services the marks are used, then to confirm that they are still in active use and determine the scope of use (channels of trade and geographic scope). A careful scrutiny of marks must also be made to see if the owners have been diligent about *policing* their marks (i.e., litigating to stop potential infringers). The litigation history can be very informative.

Finally, a report that lists the most important marks should be assessed on three key issues:

1. Can the mark be used?
2. Can the mark be registered? (This is not the same as "Can the mark be used?")

3. Is there too much dilution of the mark to gain any brand equity? For example, if the chosen mark is "Delta," there will be considerable dilution as there are hundreds of companies using the mark in addition to Delta Airlines and Delta Faucets. The mark may be ownable (Rule 1), but it may be so diluted, it can't be expanded into new fields as the company grows, violating Rule 2. (It is not OK to violate even one of the rules).

As mentioned, the answers to the first two questions are not necessarily the same. A mark may be usable, but because it is descriptive, it may not be registerable. Also, a mark may be useable *and* registerable, but it can still be weak because there are many other users, thus making it difficult to enforce or expands its use in new lines of business.

The client then must decide her/his risk tolerance. With all of these variables in play, search reports rarely come back squeaky clean. There is always some level of risk. Most often this risk comes from the possibility of an unreasonable litigant, i.e., a prior trademark owner who has proven to be "an enforcer" even in the absence of a strong legal case. If the enforcer has the money to back up their (weak) legal position, that also needs to be taken into consideration in brand selection.

It is always wise to file for federal registration, if possible, and as soon as possible. Incontestability takes five years from registration, and registration can't happen until filing.

What About Foreign Rights?

The search strategy outlined above is a good plan for clearing US trademarks. For other countries, the strategy is different.

Although most countries do not have the concept of common law rights, it is actually more difficult to get registrations in other countries. Here's why:

1. Do the math. When one has the clear title to the same trademark in multiple countries, the risk of unavailability

113

is multiplied by the number of countries where the mark is needed.

2. Foreign countries allow the registration of marks that are not actually being used (i.e., they are being warehoused), so applicants can register marks for large swaths of products/services, effectively blocking all others. This is not allowed in the US.

3. Foreign countries often reject highly suggestive marks. Since many US marks are highly suggestive, what is acceptable in the US is likely to be considered unregisterable overseas. In other words, if foreign markets are needed, stronger marks must be chosen.

4. There are trademark squatters out there! Like domain cyber-squatters, these are pirates of the trademark world. They look for up-and-coming US companies and buy the trademark rights in their home land. Then they sit back and wait.

A Strategy for Building a Global Brand

Here are the keys to having a uniform trademark in all countries:

1. Realize that a brand might not work, no matter how clever and unique it is.

2. If there is any desire to go international with the brand, international clearance should be run simultaneously with the US search. Never choose a generic, merely descriptive or descriptive mark for international use..

3. Avoid suggestive marks unless they are only tangentially suggestive. Many countries will reject those, too.

4. Find out if the word is derogatory in other languages. Start with Google translate, but don't stop there. Corrupted spellings can sound like "bad" words. The prospective words need to be sent to native speakers.

fcuk® *(French Connection U. K. – but you knew that!)*

5. Develop a strong, recognizable logo which will work worldwide and use it prominently. The following are not infringements, but examples of single brands that are not uniform worldwide, mostly because their names were already taken in some countries before the brand was expanded there:

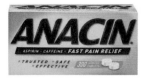

Each of the above are owned by the same company. In most cases, they couldn't get international clearance, so they had to make changes for different markets. Not a good idea, but hard to avoid.

This pair are products with the same name but from different companies. Mars (left) could not get ownership of Milky Way in the UK because it was already owned by another company.

These two have been at war for decades and consequently Budweiser (formerly USA) is not generally available in most European countries because Budvar was first in Europe.

6. Once a trademark is registered in one country, such as the US, there are **six months** to register in foreign countries and get the benefit of the first country filing date. This can

help to stop the foreign pirates who are watching the new filings at the US Trademark Office. If one files in foreign countries before the end of the six months, the foreign trademark filing is backdated to the US filing date and a pirate cannot swoop in.

The standard applied in trademark clearance searches is: Are the marks *confusingly similar?*

The ultimate test of whether there's infringement is a two-part analysis:

1. Are the words similar in *sound, appearance,* or *impression?*
2. Are the products/services in the *same channels of trade?*

For two marks to be confusingly similar, they must meet both criteria. This sounds pretty straightforward, but consider these examples:

Purina vs. (pure) Eena (brand)

This one is fictitious. It is designed to show that *clever* isn't the same as *legal*. Decision: confusingly similar. The pronunciation of the mark Pure Eena is identical to Purina. If the product wasn't so *pure*, the outcome might be different.

The "Dumb" Starbucks was not a parody. It was a coffee shop, but it didn't stay in business long. They couldn't get a food license from the city. The case never got to court, but would almost certainly be held as an infringement. If it had been a parody or a critique, and not a commercial competitor, it might have come out differently.

This one is a parody (so long as there is no film inside) and exempt: no infringement.

CHARBUCKS

This one is not a parody. Only two letters are different between the two. The court found **NO** infringement. The courts might have gotten this one wrong too. The point is that it is hard to anticipate how courts will decide trademark issues. The best policy is to avoid potential trouble when picking a mark.

The US Trademark Office found these not to be confusingly similar, despite McDonald's special super status as a famous trademark.

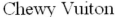

Louis Vuitton   Chewy Vuiton

Similar name but very different channels of trade. Chewy is a dog chew toy. Courts found *no* infringement, which meant no jail time for pupster. This was held to parody exception, but that opens a pandora's box of uncertainty in fair use with a commerical objective. The dog chew product is a real commercial product and could be seen as degrading to the LV brand. But the courts held otherwise. It's probably not the last word on trademark parody, so don't bank your company on this decision.

MILANZA **POTENZA**

Both are for tires. Courts found infringement. This too was a close call. The *-nza* suffix is not used by any other tire company, and Bridgestone already had Tura<u>nza</u>. There is an important lesson in this case: when a company builds a trademark portfolio of marks that share a prefix or suffix, each of the trademarks gain strength (enforceability) from the group of trademarks. Legally it's called a *family of marks*.

Takeaways for this chapter:

1. Building a brand without taking the steps to be sure it can be *owned* is brand suicide.
2. Most privately held companies think they own their brand/company name, but they actually don't. They will find out in due diligence when they try to sell, if not sooner, much to their chagrin.
3. The discovery of this lack of clear title to a brand is often made after success is achieved. NOT a good time to rebrand.
4. The US has a complex three-tier trademark system; to have clear title a brand must clear all three tiers.
5. *Confusing similarity* is the test for infringement. It is a complex legal question. Get *competent* help if faced with an infringement issue.
6. Follow Red Adair's advice: get the best legal help you can and hire a professional, not an amateur.

Chapter 6

A Rescue Plan

for brands that may *already* be in trouble

The message of this book has consistently been: a brand-centric company, built on a strong brand and great positioning, will be far more successful and enduring than one which has violated the rules. This does not mean that a strong brand will make your company succeed. If you don't have a good product or service, no brand can fix it, but if you do succeed and are brand-centric, you will grow faster, have higher profits, and create a very valuable and saleable brand. Knowing this, it makes sense to review your current brand situation.

This chapter is for those of you who, after having read this far, suspect that your existing brand(s) may already be in trouble. This might include a lot of you.

Before proceeding, you need to ask yourself this question: Am I willing to suffer the relatively lesser pain of fixing my brand problem now, or would I rather deal with a much bigger and more expensive fix later? The answer would seem to be obvious, but experience shows otherwise.

The goal of this chapter is to show that fixing the problem now is *always* worth it.

This chapter is also for those who are still struggling with the notion that a *descriptive* brand is not your friend.

Looking at the examples above, one could come away with the belief that there is nothing wrong with descriptive terms as trademarks. After all, they help *explain* what the company does, and in any case, some of these are very successful brands.

In fact, these brands are all very weak, either because they describe the product/service, describe an *attribute* of the product/service, or are tied to geography. Most of them were developed in an era when industries were protected by their governments and they really didn't have any competition, such as Air Canada and Deutsche Bank. Most of the others were simply expedient choices of marketers who wanted to avoid the work of building a real brand. Of course, if you are thinking, *Most of these brands are well known, so what is the problem?*, then you must realize that what you are **not** seeing is that the ground is littered with a *much larger* list of failed companies with descriptive names.

A brand that is tied to a product's features is not only a weak, *indefensible* brand, but it can also limit *expansion* (geographic and scope of products covered by the brand). Recall the example of Books.com vs. Amazon.com. Finally, weak trademarks are very difficult and expensive to enforce. If the key word in the brand is descriptive, even minor variations may escape infringement. Ultimately, the descriptive brand becomes diluted by the encroachment of "near" infringers, to the point that it has little or no value.

Back in the day when these two brands coexisted, how many times did a consumer purchase something from one and accidentally try to return it to the other? And the stores were not amused. They should have been. Whomever created these brands took a shortcut to brand building. There can be no brand ownership over the word "office" for office supplies, so neither company could block later sound-alike competitors.

Notice how Staples®, a much stronger brand name, was able to use "Depot" with impunity.

Fighting the Forces of Marketing Nature

Some years ago, Clorox introduced a new product category. For the last 100 years, porcelain-ware cleaners have been a combination of rocks (lava) and chlorine. The rocks scraped away the glass coating on the porcelain so that the bleach could attack the stain. Works great, but it also destroys the glass coating that prevents stains.

Clorox, which had boatloads of chlorine to spare, figured that smaller rocks and more chlorine would be safer, and it is. But what to call it?

The logic of an untrained brand marketer would say: *call it what it does* so that it does not need to be explained to the target market. Furthermore, once the product is successfully launched, *Hasta la vista, baby* – said marketer is promoted or gone. The forces of such naïve thinking can drive an otherwise smart company to make bad brand decisions. The company is then stuck with the problem long after the person who picked the name has left the building, been promoted, or works for a new company. It is the brand disaster that keeps on giving.

Options for rescue:

FIX 1: If the brand is broken, start over. This is not nearly as hard as it might sound.

> Sometimes, the best fix is to discard the weak and start over. It's not nearly as hard as you might think to start afresh, especially for companies who know their target audience and don't need to do mass marketing. Starting over is as simple as adding a *non*-descriptive **prefix** to the brand.

> If the brand is Outdoor Towels, and the company sells…well, *towels for outdoor use*, the brand could be fixed by:
>
> 1.   Adding a prefix.

2. Getting rid of the special font (i.e., admitting the "brand" is essentially the fanciful font).

WILDCOUNTRY

OUTDOOR TOWELS

3. Creating a new brand (Wild Country) and accepting that "outdoor towels" has and always will be descriptive and a weak brand.

The alternative is to continue with the broken brand and be unable to defend against another company who creates a *Quark* (brand) Outdoor Towel. When you decide to sell the company or the brand, the buyer, in due diligence, is going to tell you what you *already* know: the brand is weak and expensive or impossible to defend. In other words, it has little value.

Similar rescue procedures are needed for

127

FIX 2: Registering the brand on the SUPPLEMENTAL REGISTER of the US Trademark Office.

(The following gets quite technical; an experienced and competent trademark attorney is needed to make this work.)

Getting a federal registration of your trademark is *essential* to making the brand transferable, but it is also the best way to prevent infringement and gain national rights for the trademark.

The United State Patent and Trademark Office (USPTO) issues two kinds of trademark registrations. No other country does this. The first, "Principal Registration," is a real, empowered trademark right. The second, "Supplemental Registration," is a much weaker consolation prize. Valuable, but nothing like the real thing, though worth getting if your brand is in trouble.

In order to understand a Supplemental registration, the US Federal trademark system and its importance to brand value needs to be clarified.

Trademark Rights Pyramid

As mentioned in the last chapter, the US has a three-tier trademark system, with the federal trademark on top.

A federal trademark registration is the *gold* standard, especially if it has reached incontestability level.

A federal trademark on the Principal register has special magical properties that cannot be obtained by common law or state registrations:

1. As of the **date of filing** (not issuance), it tentatively grants *nationwide protection* to the trademark owner, subject to any *pre-existing* rights of common law users.
2. As of the date of filing, it also cuts off the **expansion** rights of a common law user, even those who have pre-existing rights.
3. Federal trademark registrations become "incontestable" after five years of registration upon filing certain documents.

These three benefits are hugely valuable. First, by being granted rights from the *filing* date, the trademark filer doesn't have to wait until the trademark application is examined and granted to *lock in* their claim to a date of first use through filing. They need to wait for the registration to be granted to exercise those rights, but the filing date is locked in.

The second benefit of a Principal federal registration is to "fence in" a common law user's expansion. As of the date of your federal trademark filing, another user cannot expand their geographic area of trademark ownership, and if their area ever shrinks, you own their lost territory.

On top of these two benefits, there is a very special third benefit that can be obtained, and it is the *gold standard* of brands. If the trademark has existed for five years (without being challenged by a third party), and the trademark registrant files certain proof documents, then the trademark registration gets a very special status: **incontestability**, which permanently prevents any pre-existing common law trademark users from challenging the trademark registration on the basis that they were the *first* user.

To recap, a federal trademark registration on the Principal register grants:

1. *Instant* national protection and prevents *expansion* of common law user rights of others.
2. Retroactive benefits to the trademark application *filing* date.
3. Incontestability – after five years, the trademark registration can't be cancelled by a prior user.

These three rights are extremely important to the *value* of the brand for reasons that are explained in the following pages.

National protection as of the *filing* date

As mentioned, common law trademark rights are created without registration, but these rights are limited to the geographic area where a company actually uses the trademark. For service providers, this is usually a local geographic area. If a company later wants to expand, their expansion may be blocked by other common law users in the expansion area or by a prior filed federal trademark registration.

The federal system eliminates the piecemeal expansion problem inherent with common law rights. If only common law rights existed, (i.e., if there was no federal registration system), then a company launching a new brand could not be assured that they would instantly have national rights, and later users/competitors could jump in and carve up the country by using the same mark in different geographic areas. This would make starting a nationwide business impossible. For example, if McDonald's had opened in Chicago, and had not filed for federal registration, a competitor, seeing McDonald's success, could open up in Los Angeles with impunity. When the original McDonald's wanted to expand to Los Angeles, it would be blocked from doing so by common law trademark rights. As you can see, the federal registration system is essential.

How common law user rights can still ruin your day (or, the importance of trademark searching)

Notice that prior common law users, i.e., users of a trademark who started before the federal trademark application was filed, do not lose their right to continue using the mark after a federal registration is granted to someone else. This means that these common law users pose a serious threat and thus the need for a comprehensive search to *find them*. In the case of Amazon, Amazon Bookstore claimed extensive geography that would have made Amazon.com's business difficult to operate since they would have been excluded from those territories. The key, therefore, is to do a very thorough search to ferret out these common law users. Surprises are definitely not good in trademark law.

Incontestability – the gold standard

Trademark incontestability is also very important. It terminates forever the right of a prior common law user to cancel a trademark registration, even if they have prior first use.

Thus it is important not only to file trademark applications often (remember the family of marks?), but also to file *early* since there is no way to accelerate the five years required for incontestability.

What if your trademark is too descriptive to be entitled to a federal registration?

There are two primary reasons why the US Trademark Office will reject a trademark application. The first is that there is a *prior filed* trademark application/registration that is too similar (i.e., "confusingly similar"). The owner of an existing registration is thrilled because the US Trademark Office will block subsequent trademark applications that are too similar at *no cost* to the prior trademark registrant. In other words, federal registration gets the US Government to do some trademark enforcement for free on behalf of the trademark owner.

The US Trademark Office will also reject a trademark application if it determines that the proposed word does not qualify as a trademark. Remember Rule 1: If *no one* can own it….? A trademark application for Beer (brand) for beer is sure to be rejected. A trademark that is generic or merely descriptive is not entitled to a federal trademark registration on the Principal register.

The rescue plan for a word that is merely descriptive is to prove to the trademark office that the word could *become* distinctive if it was so heavily marketed that users would recognize it as a trademark and not just a descriptor.

Is that even possible? Yes – it is a very risky strategy, but sometimes it works. Air Canada (the words, not the logo) for an airline that flies mostly from Canada is pretty descriptive, but with enough advertising, it has become recognizable as a trademark. Indeed, Air Canada is now considered famous. But take note: it will NEVER become a strong trademark. Other airlines are going to be able use slight variations of the words "Canada" and "Air" in combination. Indeed, *Canadian Pacific Airlines* competed with Air Canada until 2000, when it was acquired by Air Canada.

So, as a method of rescuing weak marks, massive marketing can help bring the mark back from the abyss, though nothing can fix a *generic* term. Beer for beer can never be a trademark. The rescue plan for generic is: get a *real* brand.

Even in law, there are consolation prizes.

If a trademark application is refused registration because it is merely descriptive, US law has a pretty good *consolation* prize. If the applicant can prove that the mark *could become* distinctive, the US Trademark Office will register it, but with a special limited registration certificate known as a Supplemental registration (this is Fix 2 for a broken brand).

The Supplemental registration is a consolation prize, but it's a pretty good one, considering the weakness of the proposed trademark. Unlike a Principal registration, which comes with a legal *presumption* that it is valid and enforceable, the Supplemental's enforceability requires the trademark owner to *prove* that the mark has indeed *become distinc*tive, i.e., that the public will recognize it as a trademark, before it can be enforced against an infringer. The difference is legally significant, but getting a Supplemental registration for a weak mark is a huge gift (complements of the US Congress), and a very useful right to obtain though, it is nothing like a Principal registration. Remember: this chapter is a *rescue plan*, not a best practices guide.

Remember, generic words can never become distinctive, but descriptive terms – those on the edge of the cliff, but not *off* the cliff – might be entitled to Supplemental registration. How do you know which kind of trademark you have (on or off the cliff)? You won't. Ask an experienced trademark lawyer.

Getting a Supplemental federal registration for a weak descriptive mark sounds pretty good...What's the catch? The catch is that even with a trademark registration certificate, in court, you must still prove that your trademark has acquired sufficient distinctiveness that it is recognized by the public as a trademark. (With a Principal registration, this proof is not needed). Also, a Supplemental registration can never become incontestable. It is always subject to challenge by others.

As mentioned, a Supplemental registration is only half of the prize. The other half is that once the brand gets registered, its registration stands as a block to subsequent applicants from trying to register a confusingly similar mark.

The Secret Sauce

Even though Supplemental registrations can't become incontestable, they *can* be converted into Principal registrations merely by waiting five years. The secret sauce is, **if the Supplemental registration is maintained for five years, the trademark office will normally allow an *upgrade* to a Principal registration, and a Principal registration can become incontestable.** Of course, incontestability status requires a wait of another five years (yup, that's 10 years total), but that easily beats never getting it.

If you are wondering why a weak trademark registration (Supplemental) can get an automatic upgrade to full (Principal) rights, when it really makes no sense, you are not alone. The issue was decided by the US Supreme Court (in a case involving the brand Park N Fly) some years ago and it is now the law. So, although it is never good to start with a weak brand, it is possible to take certain legal steps to prop it up. This is one of them.

Before you decide that selecting a descriptive mark isn't so bad because of these rescue options, don't forget, these are rescue procedures only. Having a life jacket doesn't make jumping off a ship in the middle of the ocean a smart move. You may not drown right away, but you are still in trouble. Likewise, if you salvage a weak mark, it still is weak. Try to break free of the temptation to repeat this mistake. Remember, The Weather Channel's victory was only partial. No one can use *The Weather Channel*, but anyone can start a cable channel with the word Weather. Furthermore, the above rescue plan takes ***ten years***. In the interim, another party may seek to cancel the registration, and then it's game over. All of that time and investment is lost.

International Warning!

If your company has ambitions of broadening the geographic scope of its trademark protection outside the United States, know this: almost none of what was stated above, about rescuing descriptive trademarks applies on the rest of this planet. Most countries, particularly those in the EU, take a dim view of descriptive marks and don't consider them available for registration. Also, no other country has a Supplemental register, so even if you are banking on this rescue plan for an international brand, it is not likely to work.

Takeaways for this chapter :

1. Get honest about your brand. If you have a broken brand, you may have to replace it.
2. It is not as hard to replace a brand as you might think.
3. Not fixing a broken brand will result in years of wasted efforts to accumulate brand equity in a bucket with no bottom.
4. There are rescue tools to patch up some damaged brands. They require legal action and time, and the clock does not start until you actually take action.

Chapter 7

Power Tools

for serious brand-centric companies

This chapter is about building a **unified** brand strategy. A unified brand strategy is one where multiple brand elements are used synergistically to create a multi-faceted brand identification.

There is more to branding than words. Most highly valuable brands are combinations of elements, such as colors and graphics. There are different ways to look at what should be branded, and tools to protect these assets.

Momentum

When a brand is working well, every subsequent product launch is so much easier, cheaper, and less risky than the first one.

When Apple introduced Apple 1, it was a struggle to gain buyer acceptance for what was essentially a circuit board in a wooden box with a funny name. It is so easy to forget that there were constant developmental steps between the Apple 1 and the iPhone, and that these weren't just technological advances – they were also brand development steps. The result: the brand as it is today. (Remember: if a business decision does not build the brand, change it so that it does.) The MacBook, introduced years after the successful Apple 2e, was built on the brand positioning of the Apple 2e (easy to use). The success of the iPhone was built on the success of the MacBook and iPod (easy to use and beautiful). When Apple Pay® was launched, it already had a running start because customers trusted Apple. That is the Apple brand at work.

No doubt you are thinking that your company does not have the resources of Apple to make your brand famous. Looking at the Apple 1, built in a garage – who would have expected that to succeed? It's not about the resources you *don't* have, it's about using what you *do* have effectively.

Notice that while Samsung is challenging Apple's dominance in smart phones, or anything else, it hasn't affected Apple's profit margins. Samsung *Pay* is not likely to get as much traction as Apple *Pay*. If success was based on the number of Samsung phones in use, it should be easy for Samsung to dominate in the electronics payment business, but it never will because its brand connection to the customer is not as strong.

It's about the brand.

Apple has cultivated a long history of trust with its customers. Its brand positioning is rock solid. Samsung's is still a work in progress.

Defending your brand against copyists

The first function of a strong brand is to collect and hold the accruing brand equity. The second function of a brand/trademark, particularly registered trademarks, is to stop competitors from stealing the brand equity (i.e., goodwill) you have worked hard to obtain.

If you build a unified brand strategy which connects multiple brand elements, it becomes that much harder for competitors to copy your brand.

This chapter is about sophisticated and powerful, but less well-known, brand tools. They are not hard to use, and the benefits are large, but *timing* is key.

Here are five powerful brand tools, each of which will be discussed in this chapter:

1. Graphics (logos) as trademarks
2. Color as a trademark
3. Product shape trademarks (2D/3D)
4. Design patents as placeholders for product shape trademarks

5. Methods and features as trademarks

Graphics (Logos) as Trademarks

It's easy to see the power of a graphic, but what is important to realize is that *these are trademarks in their own right*, not just word-mark *helpers*.

Note how these strong brands don't actually need their word marks to get the brand message across. Also, these graphics are legally strong in that they are not descriptive. None of these *describes* any aspect of the product.

The rules of owning logos/graphics are pretty much the same as the rules for owning words.

Merely descriptive/generic logos are not brands. They can't be owned. They don't accumulate brand equity. They are a complete waste of time. Therefore a photo of an apple for apple pies is merely descriptive. But if you take that actual apple photo and make it a little funky, then it is no longer merely descriptive. It becomes *ownable, but only with respect to the unique apple caricature*. It will always be a weak trademark for apple pies.

But the same stylized apple logo, applied to *music recordings,* is a strong trademark because for music it is not descriptive at all.

So as with words, strong logos/graphics build strong equity.

The hidden danger of logos

Logos, however, have a special weakness: they are often not perceived as "real" brands by their brand owners. Consequently, they get **changed too often** and lose their brand equity.

Why are they changed so often? Their owners get tired of them. Sometimes the changes are dramatic and probably necessary (as seen with the 1984 Apple logo change), and sometimes they are evolutionary, as with Shell. Evolutionary change in logo is best because radical change is the same as starting from zero again.

Starbucks: An Illustrated History

Evolutionary is best.

OK, Apple's first logo was pretty crazy, but after changing it in 1984, they've kept the apple shape (with leaf and bite) the same. They gave up the color band in 1998, which was a major departure, and in 2010 they went for "shiny," which is currently in vogue. It is likely that they are not done making evolutionary changes.

Generally speaking, radical and frequent change is not a good idea. Logos/graphics are far more susceptible to unnecessary change (called "updating" or "freshening up") than word marks, because it is believed that logos are not as important as word marks. *This is a serious brand mistake.*

The Nike swoosh is a perfect example of a logo becoming *more important* than the word mark. The swoosh is clearly not descriptive (though it abstractly suggests motion). Most importantly, it carries the brand in all languages, and for an international company, this is a huge advantage.

Even though a graphic brand can be a company's most valuable brand, they are often killed by *change mongers* who wish to "freshen up" the logo/graphic. Often, the freshening up is a wholesale destruction of the graphical trademark. Brands don't easily adapt to changes, so it is important that any change be made with extreme care to maintain the original brand and the value it has accumulated.

Warning: Ownership of logos/graphics is more complex than ownership of words.

Unlike words, logos (graphics) are subject to *copyright* protection, so it is critically important that you know whether you own the logo that you paid for. The basic rule of copyright ownership in the US (whose copyright laws are unlike any other country's) is that you DON'T end up owning what you've paid for. Yes, that's right: you don't automatically own the graphic you commissioned unless it falls into a very special Work For Hire rule or you get an assignment of rights. The Work for Hire rule is very complex, so suffice it to say, get legal help on this one. Some basic information is located here: https://www.reellawyers.com/michael-lasky/copyright-works-hire/.

The easiest way a logo strategy is messed up is when the freelance graphic designer *steals* someone else's graphic (without anyone knowing) to use for your logo. That's copyright infringement, and when your company is caught with the stolen graphic, you will have to stop using the graphic (after paying attorney's fees and damages). All of the brand equity in the graphic goes down the drain. It is very ugly. Very embarrassing. Pretty easy to avoid.

Here's how it can happen:

1. A graphic artist is commissioned to make a logo.

2. The artist looks at Google images for ideas and makes a modification of some existing image.
3. A "derivative work" is produced, which is a copyright infringement.
4. Years later, when the logo is valuable, the original author discovers and challenges it.
5. The logo must then be changed.
6. US copyright law grants attorney's fees and very high damages. The sum of all of those damage can easily put a small company out of business.
7. Brand value is erased.

It can also happen this way:

1. A graphic artist is commissioned to produce a graphic. The company does not get a written assignment of the work from the artist (i.e., a document which transfers ownership rights to you).
2. The logo is paid for and a receipt given.

In this scenario, under US copyright law, the company only owns the copy of the graphic it was given. It can't reproduce further copies, post on the Internet, etc. Crazy? Maybe, but it's the law. See: ***Community for Creative Non-Violence v. Reid***, 490 U.S. 730 (1989), decided by the US Supreme Court on facts similar to the scenario above.

The right way (it's called *clean room* technique):

1. The artist is told, in words, generally what to design, but is not shown any other graphics.
2. The artist is instructed as follows:
   a. You may browse Google images for ideas, but do NOT copy any specific images.
   b. Only make written notes of what elements you like, not whole images.
   c. Create your graphic without direct access to any other images.
   d. Use your imagination; don't create a derivative of someone else's graphic.

3. Of course, get an assignment of IP rights directly from the artist, not his/her company. Directly. If the artist works for a company, get an assignment from them also. Under US law, it is difficult to know which will be effective, so get both.

This *clean room* method shields your company from a claim of copyright infringement. If your company is charged with infringement, the designer will be asked the following question: What techniques did you employ to prevent access to the infringed graphic? The correct answer for him/her is to be able to honestly recite, "I followed a four-step method to deliberately prevent myself from accidently copying the works of others."

What if the designer's graphic is a dead-on copy of someone else's, but he/she didn't see that other graphic? It is, as a matter of law, NOT a copyright infringement. Infringement requires copying. If it was not copied, even if it looks similar, it can't be an infringement.

On the flip side, there are things you can do to protect your valuable graphic/logo from being copied:

1. **Register the graphic** as a copyright with the US copyright office.
2. Insert small, virtually unnoticeable irregularities into the graphic, so if it is copied, the irregularity will appear in the copy. An example would be a small error in a line in the graphic. The error will provide proof of copying, the evidence needed to prove copyright infringement.

The important takeaway with respect to graphics: **a logo/graphic is a separate trademark**. It must have its own federal trademark registration separate from the word brand. If you're trying to save money by registering the composite mark (word + graphic), what happens when it seems necessary to "update" the logo? The entire trademark registration cannot be renewed – and the word mark in the composite registration is lost at the same time! This results in loss of the filing date and the all-important trademark *incontestability* protection (see Chapter 5). That would be a colossal trademark train wreck.

"Freshening up" a brand may also be kissing valuable brand equity goodbye. Be sure the *customers* think it is stale before taking action. Remember, customers/clients are comforted by stability and consistency.

Campbell's soup cans have evolved (left 1869, right 2010), but very slowly. The San Andreas fault moves faster. The new soup can design still is dominated by a red banner and the same stylized font. Yes, there are changes, but they are subtle. It's a fresher look, but it's still the familiar brand.

Old Spice has dramatically changed its fortunes by changing its target demographic. Instead of targeting elderly seamen, it now seeks the under 30 market. Most of the heavy lifting was done by smart marketing, and the logo changed only slightly. The color red was maintained, the ship got a lot more sleek, but it is still a boat. It is unlikely that they lost a single member of the *old* demographic with these changes, and the new demographic didn't even know there was a change.

The French car maker Peugeot has had a lot of trouble staying with the same graphic image. In 1998, it made a major change in its brand by adding the blue background and simplifying the lion. It lasted 12 years. Then they gave up one of the most distinctive elements of the brand: blue. (At least the lion didn't become extinct, too.) They gave up a lot when they gave up the blue color.

The moral: use caution when assuming that the brand image is tired. A graphic overhaul is the same as making a graphic brand walk the plank. What is the driving force for the change? Is it because there is a new marketer/agency? Be worried if your new agency's mantra is: *Whatever the last guy did is wrong.* A successful and strong brand can last for the life of the company. It must not be hijacked by transient independent contractors, who are unconcerned with brand continuity. The rule of thumb is, by the time you are sick and tired of your graphic image, the customer base is just beginning to recognize it.

Color as a Trademark

Color can be a critical part of your brand, but as you might expect, there are rules which must be followed to make color ownable (remember Rule 2: If you don't own it, it is of no value to you).

Similarly, when companies want to "freshen up" a color, that means changing it to another color, and that means doom for the color being recognized as a symbol of the company. So if you are going to build a truly powerful brand, you need to get a blood oath from the company not to get bored. For years, if not decades.

Sometimes people are only vaguely aware of the power of color as a trademark, but it is nevertheless absolutely clear that it is working on our brains.

When an ugly brown truck pulls up to the house, why are we always delighted? Because it is clearly UPS. Yes, the brown UPS color is unattractive, but there is still a positive reaction to its appearance. That is because UPS brown has a *second meaning* (besides ugly). It means something we want has arrived. Thus brown = happiness. Brands aren't supposed to be pretty. They only need to be *memorable*.

When will UPS change the color of its vans? If they are smart, the answer is NEVER. Are they bored with it? I am sure they have been bored with it for decades, but someone in the company, the Brand Czar, made it clear that brown was a sacred company asset and, like the crown jewels, it must not be given up, no matter what the next agency says.

Every company needs a Brand Czar with the foresight to see the value of using color as a brand and the power to keep others from changing it in the name of a *freshening up.*

Color as a brand: the rules

Not every use of color makes a brand.

To be a brand, the color must meet two requirements:

1) The color may not be **functional**.
2) The color must be used consistently and long enough for the public to make the brand association. That is, until the color has **acquired a distinctive connection** with the company.

But what is a *functional* color?

A functional color is one which is necessary or helpful to the use of the product.

Orange/red/yellow are colors of safety. They help make things more visible. Used on products which need visibility, these colors can never be brands. They are functional.

One could argue that brown for trucks is functional because it helps to keep them from looking dirty. That might be true for a "dirt" color, but brown is not specifically functional for that purpose. That was also not the reason for UPS's decision. Rather, brown was the color of prestigious Pullman rail coaches of the day.

Acquired distinctiveness in the mind of the public

Assuming it's not a functional color, it still has to meet the second requirement: CONSISTENT USE until the color is *associated* with the company. This is where most color branding strategies fail. The company sees *consistent* color as boring and are driven to change the color from year to year.

Consider this: fiberglass insulation is transluscent when manufactered. It is dyed to suit the manfucturer's desire. Most insulation is yellow.

When a house is being built, during the frameup phase, the insulation is exposed. If the house is wrapped in *Owens Corning* insulation, it is always PINK. ALWAYS. It screams, This house used Owens Corning fiberglass.

150

Simultaneously, Owens Corning uses the Pink Panther to say, "You know it is our brand when you see pink."

Look at what they get: the product is viewed by thousands of passersby and without a word, it says: *Another house built with OWENS CORNING.*

What is the cost of adding pink dye to fiberglass over yellow? Pretty much nothing.It can't be sold without some color because it would be too dangerous to install. Owens Corning's stroke of genius was to deviate from the standard issue color – yellow.

What is the *cost benefit* of a color screaming your brand day in, day out? Priceless. Owens Corning had great foresight to have color-branded fiberglass. Would your company have been willing to make such a move and stayed with it long enough to get brand traction?

Oh, yes, don't forget the Pink Panther. Corning doubled down on making people remember pink by taking a trademark license for a movie charater.

Here's another example of a company that successfully made color part of their brand: John Deere.

When farmers buy attachments for their tractors, they can buy other brands because the hitch and power take-off are all standardized. But they can't buy an attachment, which is *John Deere green* unless it is made by John Deere. Amazingly, farmers have a strong preference for attachments which are color-coordinated. Deere makes a lot of tractors. That gives it a leg up on attachments because their colors match. If you want a matched set, all of the pieces are going to have to come from Deere. When you see a tractor at 500 meters, you know immediately if it is a Deere. The color speaks the brand. A long line of marketers have possibly urged the company to "freshen up" the color. They must have a Brand Czar who is a pro.

Now compare Caterpiller. Yellow for earth moving equipment is functional. It helps people see the machine, so Caterpiller probably didn't have the latitude to use a different color.

Instead, they shortened the name and made the letters visible for miles. That works.

This next example is harder for some people to understand. This pair of shoes costs around $1,400 ($700 each, if that makes you feel any

152

better). They are nice shoes. Even *really* nice. Well-made and superbly styled. The material cost is probably $50. Labor perhaps another $100. So where is the other $1250? Of course, a lot of wholesalers along the way are taking a chunk, but that still won't explain the retail price. What makes them worth more than other shoes and totally identifiable is their fire-engine red soles. The company owns *red* soles for luxury shoes, and it is certainly working. Their annual revenue growth rate is 40%! They can't make shoes fast enough. They could raise their prices and their profits would not drop.

The company is, of course, Louboutin of France. They just won a lawsuit against YSL to establish their exclusive trademark right on red soles. Every time a customer takes a step, the soles shout the brand. They are saying: "I just paid $1400 for these shoes, and now you know." (Many of us will never get it. Just realize that it totally works.)

What if Louboutin had used red one year and green another, and blue this year? *They could not claim ownership of red.* Consistent use is requried by law to make a claim of brand ownership. The company must believe in the color as a brand and stick with it until they are sick of it – and then keep using it. No freshening up. Color is hard to establish as a distinctive brand, so any changes may reset the brand clock to zero.

Imagine going back in time and speaking with Christian Louboutin. He is going to market a prestige/luxury shoe product. It is beautiful to look at. But now, he is going to draw attention *away* from the shoe uppers by painting the soles a distracting red. Would you have advised him that this move will make his shoes sell faster than he can make them and bring him fabulous weath? Or would you have told him that he was crazy?

A company must have the nerve to chose a color scheme and promote it as a point of brand recognition. Louboutin is a case in point – the red sole does not detract from the shoe; rather it vastly (counter-intuitively) enhances its cachet and asking price.

The power of color as a brand is not just limited to shoes and tractors.

Drug makers also cash in on color.

If it is purple, it is Nexium. If it is light blue and diamond-shaped, it is Viagra. Interestingly, when Viagra went generic in the UK, Pfizer sold a white diamond version at a lower price than the blue diamond. Chemically, the two were no different. Yet, the blue ones fetch a higher price.

These arches are ALWAYS yellow (except in Sedona, Arizona, where they are required to be teal to fit with the landscape).

If the product can't be made a unique color because it is made of precious metal, how about the package? Tiffany Blue. It says, *I spent too much, but you are worth it.*

Shape as a Trademark

Even more recognizable than color is *shape*. It too can be a trademark, and there are two kinds of shape trademarks:

1. The shape of **packaging,** and
2. The shape of the **product**.

The shape of packaging is relatively easy to get registered as a trademark. The shape of the product itself as a trademark is very difficult, but far from impossible. It requires the same special ingredient as color: acquired distinctiveness, or recognition by the public that the color belongs to your company.

Three-dimensional products

Perrier is both a color and shape trademark. Coke is shape only. It is a bit unclear whether the bottle is a *package* or a *product*, but the courts would say it is a product with an integrated package, so getting ownership falls under the higher standard for *products*.

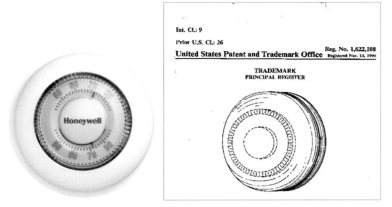

The Honeywell thermostat has a long history. Invented in the 1950s, it is still in use, and replacements, both analog and digital, are also available from Honeywell.

Honeywell filed for utility (functional) patents and design patents. Both have long expired, but Honeywell realized two things about their product: 1) it was very well known, and 2) there was still a huge secondary (i.e., replacement) market for the round shape.

One of the reasons why homeowners wanted a replacement round thermostat is "paint archeology," i.e., when house painters encounter a thermostat, they never remove it, but rather just paint around it. After 20 years or so, there are millimeters of paint built up, and now the only replacement thermostat that will fit the paint archeology is a *round* one of the same diameter.

Honeywell knew that there was no way to extend a patent, but they could potentially get *a product configuration* trademark, i.e., a trademark on the way the product *looks*.

A product configuration trademark is obtainable on a 3D object (or a 2D computer interface) if the object is:

    a)   Non-functional (same test as for color).

    b)   Has *acquired distinctiveness*, i.e., the public would recognize it as being a particular company's product.

In order to help prove that the mark was distinctive, consumer survey results were submitted to the trademark office, and to emphasize the distinctive feature of the product Honeywell called it The Round™. Hopefully, you will realize after reading this far that "The Round" is a pretty weak trademark because it describes an aspect of the product. However, in Honeywell's case, it was a worthwhile sacrifice in order to draw attention to this distinguishing (round) feature.

For a functional product like a thermostat, it wasn't easy to prove that being round was non-functional. We (I worked on the case) also needed to prove that it was not financially advantageous to make the thermostat round. It was shown that, in fact, it was more difficult and expensive to make a round thermostat than a square one, and that a high percentage of the public recognized round as relating to Honeywell (i.e., acquired distinctiveness). The US Trademark Office granted a trademark registration.

Years later, Honeywell's trademark rights were lost as a result of an adverse court ruling on functionality, but they *did* get to extend their rights for 20+ years. Not a bad outcome.

Hershey recently got its chocolate bar shape registered as a trademark.

Williams Sonoma sold a brownie baking pan which made brownies in a shape similar to the Hershey bar, but the word **Hershey** was replaced with word **CHOCOLATE** embossed in the pan, presumably so as not to infringe the word brand. Hershey sued. The case has been settled, and the Williams Sonoma baking pan is off the market. Hershey made their point.

Nylon pantyhose don't have much of a shape. Rather, they enhance the user's shape. On the shelf, pantyhose are usually packaged in blah flat packs. Until L'eggs came on the market. L'eggs (now Hanes) used packaging which made the brand instantly famous. The package was an oversized egg, which was wildly distinctive. Sadly, they found that the egg shape could not be packed densely enough and they *gave up* the only differentiator they had. Now their packaging is just like everyone else's...blah. Perhaps they could have solved the density problem with better point of sale engineering and kept their key differentiator. Clearly, they lacked a Brand Czar who would have protected them from trashing their most important differentiator.

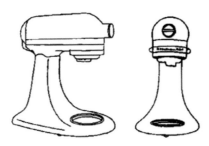

KitchenAid (Whirlpool) has obtained a trademark in the US and Europe on the shape of their mixer stand (not including the bowl). The product has been produced in the millions and is recognized as a KitchenAid brand.

Whirlpool's mixer   Kenwood's mixer

In Europe, KitchenAid sued Kenwood – not on the basis of a patent, but their trademark. KitchenAid said that it has litigated this trademark over 80 times successfully, but this time it lost on functionality. The EU is very strict, much more so than the US on products whose shapes are *partially* functional. This case was never litigated in the US, but US courts would likely have ruled the opposite. After all, the KitchenAid design was totally revolutionary. The product could be made with an entirely different form, but competitors know that it will be easier to sell if they follow the leader's design.

Two dimensional products – computer interfaces and icons can also be trademarks

It would be incorrect to assume that a trademark can't be obtained based on the look of the product if it is flat, i.e., two dimensional. Computer program interfaces and the icons themselves are protectable as product configuration trademarks even though they are two dimensional. They only need to meet the same two rules that apply to 3D products and packaging: 1) non-functional, and 2) recognized by users and being distinctive (acquired distinctiveness).

Thus two dimensional products require the same willingness to keep the *look and feel* of the interface the same from version to version. In other words, *don't freshen up*.

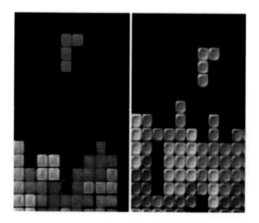

In this lawsuit, Tetris was able to assert that the little colored squares of Mino were a trademark infringement. (By the way, they also found *copyright* infringement by Xio.)

Here are the key elements of *product configuration trademarks* (PCTs):

1. PCTs cover a non-functional feature of a product or interface.
2. PCTs are hard to get because proof of acquired distinctiveness is hard to amass.
3. It's important to be willing to continue with the same shape for a long time, even if it seems boring.
4. **PCTs are very vulnerable** during their early years to competitors who copy the shape, i.e., before the product shape has achieved "acquired distinctiveness."
5. A PCT trademark, once obtained, can last forever

Combining a PCT with a word and color brand will make your brand vastly more valuable and powerful.

Closing the vulnerability gap

A key element in getting a product configuration trademark (PCT) is proving that the shape is known by the public as being distinct, i.e., it has acquired recognizability as a *shape*.

If competitors copy the shape in that intervening period, it will NEVER get acquired distinctiveness. During that period, there is a vulnerability gap.

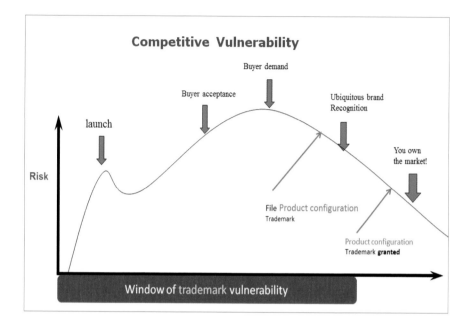

Why not file to register a PCT trademark at product launch? It can't be done. The product shape does not yet have *acquired* distinctiveness. Until it does, there is no protection on the shape. Thus, the gap may be very long.

There is a Fix: *Design Patents*

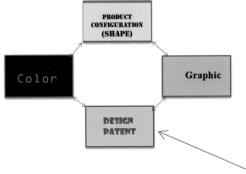

In 2012, the Apple vs. Samsung patent infringement case was decided in favor of Apple. It was a pivotal case in intellectual property law. Apple was awarded $1 billion by the jury against Samsung. It wasn't a patent case in the traditional sense.

Apple sued Samsung for copying the look of the iPhone 3 on the basis of PCTs and *design* patents. Basically, they doubled down by filing for both kinds of protection, PCT trademark and design patent, even though they pretty much cover the same subject matter.

The issue, at trial, was simply this: would an *ordinary observer* believe that the Samsung Galaxy looked substantially like the iPhone 3? The core of Samsung's argument was that a *flat brick* isn't distinctive enough to be a trademark, and not novel enough to be entitled to a design patent. Apple was able to make the argument that up until the iPhone, all phones were anything but flat. They had keyboards, they flipped, they had complicated shapes, but they weren't flat bricks. Apple's breakthrough was that they threw out all of the conventions of the past and created something new and recognizable.

The market loved it, and they noticed it at Samsung HQ in Seoul, where it was determined that a *flat* brick was the thing to have.

The jury was interviewed after the trial, and, amongst other reasons, what apparently won the day was *quantity*. Apple's number of design patents plus registered product configuration trademarks was too much for the jury to ignore. While Samsung had argued that all of the registered patents and trademarks were invalid, the jury couldn't accept that the US Patent and Trademark Office had been wrong *seven* times (there were three trademark registrations and four design patents) when they granted the registrations and patents in the first place.

An obvious takeaway is: the more pieces of registered intellectual property you own, the more likely you are to keep your competitors out of the market.

On appeal, the court *invalidated* the product configuration trademarks (PCTs) on complex functionality grounds, but upheld the design patents and awarded Apple $650 million!

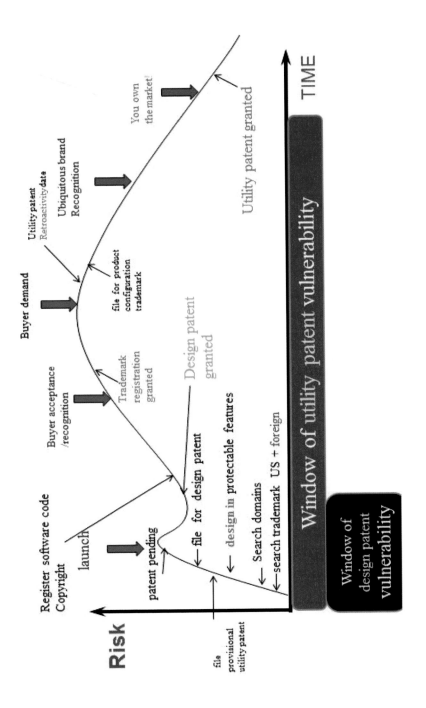

The takeaway from this is clear: PCTs are very valuable, but they have to be used in tandem with design patents or the shape may be copied during the vulnerability period. In PCT trademarks, that period can last from two to five years. Design patents can often be obtained in 18 months or, with accelerated procedure, fewer.

Design patents are the *place holder* for PCT trademark protection; they "hold the fort" until the acquired distinctiveness cavalry arrives. Design patents last 15 years, so that should be more than enough time to cover a PCT's vulnerability gap. Together, there is ownership (i.e., transferable value) of a product configuration with less risk that competitors will copy the shape/interface/icon before it becomes eligible for PCT protection.

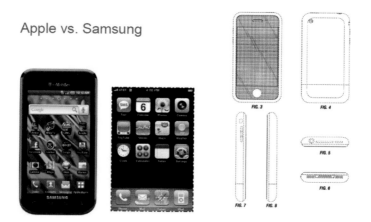

Apple vs. Samsung

So why doesn't everyone use this design patent-to-PCT strategy? Actually, all the really smart brand-based companies do. The number of design patent filings since the Apple v. Samsung decision has tripled. It's an advanced strategy, but easy to implement.

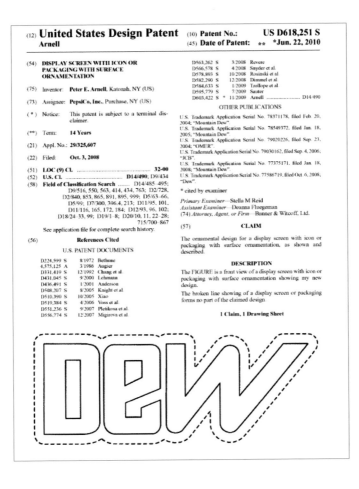

(12) **United States Design Patent**
Arnell

(10) Patent No.: **US D618,251 S**
(45) Date of Patent: ** *Jun. 22, 2010

(54) **DISPLAY SCREEN WITH ICON OR PACKAGING WITH SURFACE ORNAMENTATION**

(75) Inventor: **Peter E. Arnell**, Katonah, NY (US)

(73) Assignee: **PepsiCo, Inc.**, Purchase, NY (US)

(*) Notice: This patent is subject to a terminal disclaimer.

(**) Term: **14 Years**

(21) Appl. No.: **29/325,607**

(22) Filed: **Oct. 3, 2008**

(51) LOC (9) Cl. **32-00**
(52) U.S. Cl. **D14/490**; D9/434
(58) Field of Classification Search D14/485-495; D9/516, 550, 563, 414, 434, 763; D2/728, D2/840, 853, 865, 891, 895, 999; D5/63-66, D5/99; D7/300, 396.4, 213; D11/95, 101, D11/116, 165, 172, 184; D12/93, 96, 102; D18/24-33, 99; D19/1-8; D20/10, 11, 22-28; 715/700-867
See application file for complete search history.

(56) **References Cited**

U.S. PATENT DOCUMENTS

D224,599 S	8/1972	Bethune
4,575,125 A	3/1986	Augier
D331,419 S	12/1992	Chang et al.
D431,045 S	9/2000	Lehmann
D436,491 S	1/2001	Anderson
D508,207 S	8/2005	Knight et al.
D510,390 S	10/2005	Xiao
D519,384 S	4/2006	Voss et al.
D551,236 S	9/2007	Pletikosa et al.
D556,774 S	12/2007	Migirova et al.
D563,262 S	3/2008	Revere
D566,578 S	4/2008	Snyder et al.
D578,893 S	10/2008	Rosinski et al.
D582,290 S	12/2008	Dimmel et al.
D584,633 S	1/2009	Trollope et al.
D595,779 S	7/2009	Sauter
D603,422 S *	11/2009	Arnell D14/490

OTHER PUBLICATIONS

U.S. Trademark Application Serial No. 78371178, filed Feb. 20, 2004; "Mountain Dew".
U.S. Trademark Application Serial No. 78549372, filed Jan. 18, 2005; "Mountain Dew".
U.S. Trademark Application Serial No. 79020226, filed Sep. 23, 2004; "OMER".
U.S. Trademark Application Serial No. 79030162, filed Sep. 4, 2006; "JCB".
U.S. Trademark Application Serial No. 77375171, filed Jan. 18, 2008; "Mountain Dew".
U.S. Trademark Application Serial No. 77586719, filed Oct. 6, 2008; "Dew".

* cited by examiner

Primary Examiner—Stella M Reid
Assistant Examiner—Deanna Fluegeman
(74) Attorney, Agent, or Firm—Banner & Witcoff, Ltd.

(57) **CLAIM**

The ornamental design for a display screen with icon or packaging with surface ornamentation, as shown and described.

DESCRIPTION

The FIGURE is a front view of a display screen with icon or packaging with surface ornamentation showing my new design.

The broken line showing of a display screen or packaging forms no part of the claimed design.

1 Claim, 1 Drawing Sheet

PepsiCo has obviously registered the *trademark* for DEW, but the image above is not a trademark registration. It is a design patent on the stylized words. In this case, they may have done so for another very important reason: infringement damages.

In trademark infringement, the amount of damages obtainable from the infringer is usually based on the *actual* damage to the brand. This requires complex proof. In design patent law, the damage calculation is for **all of the profits** relating to the product which infringes the design. In other words, the damages for infringing a design patent are: *How much money did you make? Hand it over.*

Ouch. That can be a big number.

A warning about design patents:

A trap for the unwary. All patents, including design patents, have **time limits** and other special requirements for filing. If you miss the time limit, the chance to file is gone forever.

Generally speaking, the limits are:

1. A design patent must be filed before the design is made public for international protection or within one year of public disclosure for the US. If the applicant doesn't make those dates, they can **never** file. This means that to be a brand pro, one has to file design patents *on speculation*, i.e., before the product is a hit.
2. A design patent must meet the requirements of novelty and non-obviousness rules. This is pretty easy for design, but it means that if your PCT design is the same as something already in the public domain, it can't be patented.

Most design patents are *incorrectly* filed and provide an easy workaround. The patent office will grant your design patent without telling you its flaws. It's not their problem. Hire a patent attorney who has filed *a lot* of design patents (not utility patents) **and** litigated a few. They will know how to get it right. As you can see, this is very complicated. You will need a skilled patent attorney who knows, really, *really* knows, designs.

The takeaway is: in planning for a brand to succeed, it's important to take action to protect it in as many ways as are available.

Methods and Features as Trademarks

Perhaps the most underutilized, and most powerful, brand tool is to protect *methods* and *features* of the product/service in addition to the product itself. Products come and go, but features of the product or service may live much longer and hence become more valuable.

The ad above has five trademarks:

1. Progressive (word)
2. Flo (the person)
3. Name Your Price®
4. The barcode scanner
5. The blue and white color scheme

Name Your Price® is a registered trademark for the *method* of calculating the cost of insurance. It is a feature trademark and it is really simple. It says, "Tell me what you have in your wallet, and we'll find a way to make that into an insurance premium." It is a *method or feature* of the main product, insurance.

Admittedly, Name Your Price® is a weak trademark, but it is not the core trademark of the company. It was registered after proving that the trademark had acquired sufficient distinctiveness through massive marketing.

As a feature, it can be used with *any* insurance product which Progressive creates, so it will probably be around for a long time. Notice that it is closely associated with a barcode scanner, which, in effect, could also become a trademark for Progressive.

Ford understood the importance of branding features to emphasize their significance.

Consider that a car with a smart phone interface...is just a car with a smart phone interface. SYNC is exactly that, a smart phone interface. But as a branded feature, it draws *attention* to itself and makes the feature important. It also makes it easier to explain, and once customers are familiar with it, they will refer to it as Ford Sync, but they mean *Ford Sync (brand), a car with a smart phone interface*. SYNC, the brand, makes that long story short and easy to remember. That's what brands do.

General Motors did something similar. What is OnStar? A device that is built into the car and that can call for help automatically if it detects an accident (and more). That explanation requires a lot of words. OnStar – much shorter.

By the way, since the generic phrase *-a device which can call for help automatically if it detects an accident condition-* is so awful, the competition wants to call it "something like OnStar." By doing that, the competition is saying, "OnStar is the real deal, but please buy ours." How well does that work?

GM should be pleased with that headline.

The competition uses the following names: Mercedes: MBRACE; BMW: ASSIST; Lexus: ENFORM; Toyota: SAFETY CONNECT; Hyundai: BLUE LINK; Infiniti: CONNECTION.

What a sad group of names. You can almost hear the echo of car salespeople saying, "Works just like OnStar..."

The moral: get there first, create a strong brand, create a challenging generic term to go with it, and make the competition sweat.

Takeaways for this chapter:

1. A unified brand strategy is a kit of brand tools which give brands synergy.
2. A branding pro will use *all* of the tools available.
3. Color, graphics, and shapes are powerful trademark tools which are frequently overlooked but can make the brand and company uber-valuable.
4. If your company doesn't have a Brand Czar to resist the forces which want to destroy the brands by "freshening them up," appoint yourself. This is crucial.
5. Design patents play a big role in filling the vulnerability gap in the time it takes to get acquired distinctiveness.
6. Branding *methods* and *features* is a smart brand strategy because these features are often used on multiple products without becoming obsolete. Remember Dolby Labs?

Chapter 8

Renting Instead of Buying

How brand licensing can save you years of brand building

While renting TVs and furniture is usually a bad idea, very often renting a *brand* can be a good strategy for becoming instantly brand-centric. For some companies, it is a matter of needing a fast launch into fame. For others, renting saves the cost of building the infrastructure to manage a brand strategy. For pretty much everyone, the numbers speak for themselves: if you can license the right brand, the cost benefit is almost always worth the trouble.

Brand rental, more commonly known as *brand licensing*, is using a previously established brand and leveraging its success with your product or service. At first blush, it would seem to make no sense to rent a brand, because at the end of the day, the renter never owns anything. However, in the case of brands, that is not necessarily true. It depends on the terms of the license. It's possible to rent in perpetuity. It is also possible to license a brand and then migrate to your own brand. One thing that's certain: a brand license can shave years off the difficult task of brand building.

Some years ago, the automotive department at Target got a makeover. They were selling a range of auto supplies under the Target® brand. Consider the humble oil filter. An oil filter is a cheap auto part, in the range of $3-5; meanwhile a new car may cost $40,000+. There are those who like to change their own oil for fun or to save money (and obviously a lot of people do, or there wouldn't be oil filters for sale at Target and Wal-Mart). Oil filters are deceptively important. If the oil filter fails, the car could be completely ruined and the warranty voided.

So here is the buyer's dilemma when shopping for a filter. Let's say the Target brand oil filter costs $3 and the FRAM brand filter is $5. The car costs $40k. Are you going to save two bucks on a Target brand filter? It is not just a math problem, it is a trust (or brd) question. FRAM is in the oil filter business. They have a strong desire to prove that they make quality filters. Target is not in the oil filter business. They subcontracted making the filter out to someone. There is no way to know how dedicated to quality this unnamed sub-contractor is. Did Target choose the best manufacturer of oil filters? Have they changed sub-contractors recently? Does the Target filter have filter paper or toilet paper inside? (It is unlikely, but still gives one pause.) The message of the Target *brand* with respect to oil filters is, pretty much a mystery. The ultimate question to ask is, How did Target get the price of their filter below the price point of FRAM? Did they reduce their margins or quality, or both? You don't and can't know.

Target needed a way to solve the problem of house brands for *technical* products where quality could not be visually measured by the customer but yet there were are serious consequences to buying a product of

175

unknown quality. For liquid hand soap, not such a big deal, but for the family car, that is another matter.

CAR AND DRIVER

Enter CAR AND DRIVER brand. Car and Driver (C&D) is a magazine which has been around for a long time and has a strong brand history of reviewing everything automotive. But, *they don't make oil filters*. They don't make anything other than magazines. But they do have a standard of quality to uphold, and Target brilliantly leveraged that.

Target took a brand license from C&D. Target pays a percentage royalty to C&D for use of the brand. Such royalties are typically 2-10% for the right to use the brand on specific goods. The licensee (Target) also promises C&D that the sub-contractor who makes the filters will make them to a standard acceptable to C&D. We can't know if they agreed to a high standard of quality, but if they didn't, it would tarnish the C&D brand. At least the promise is one of consistency; a C&D/Target filter purchased one month is very likely to be of the same quality the next month. That is the *brand promise*, and it is important and valuable to the buyer.

So, back to our buyer who confronts the Target shelf with these four brands at the following (fictitious) price points:

Toyota $8

FRAM $6

Car and Driver $5

Target $4

Here's how a consumer might size up the choices. Toyota: they make good cars and are responsible for their warranties. They need to make great filters or they will be making expensive warranty repairs. But $8 is a lot. FRAM: they don't make cars but they are filter experts. I can trust them. Car and Driver: I didn't think they made filters, but the magazine is solid and I don't think they would put their name on an inferior product. Target: I love Target stores, but what do they know about oil filters?

The customer with a rusted out junker might have made a beeline to the Target brand, but that's not Target's preferred customer anyway. The customer with a more valuable car (Target's preferred customer) will choose one of the others. Will they chose C&D? Very likely, but for sure they will choose C&D more often than they would have chosen the Target brand.

From Target's point of view, the most valuable commodity they have is *shelf space*. If they can turn that space 1.5x or 2x faster by paying a 5% royalty to C&D, and they make more margin on C&D (even after royalty), then it's a complete no brainer.

And that's actually how it works. Licensing is often a complete no brainer for most companies. The trick is to find the right brand and get them to license to you on terms that work. That is the hard part.

Who will grant a suitable license?

In the oil filter story, if FRAM had granted Target a license, that would have been a home run, but of course, FRAM would never do that.

The genius of Target's license of C&D is that C&D has a great reputation, but they don't compete in the oil filter space. C&D is merely stretching their brand. On the other hand, C&D, as licensor, has taken a big risk. If the quality of the filters is too low, it will damage their brand. C&D has a strong interest in the filters sold under its brand being of good quality.

After the bankruptcy of Polaroid, its brand was sold off to different companies of varying quality. Petters Group Worldwide bought most of the Polaroid brand for over $400 million. The deal was highly successful for Petters. Everyone knew that Polaroid was out of business, but they still respected the brand. The Polaroid brand was particularly valuable because it spoke to innovation, even if that innovation happened 50 years ago and is now obsolete. In 2014, the Polaroid brand rights again changed hands, but the public was largely unaware that it was not the original Polaroid company venturing into new territory.

Recall the example of Owens Corning (OC) pink in the section of Chapter 7 concerning color trademarks. There's even more to that story. OC started dying their fiberglass pink in 1953 to provide visual contrast. In 1985 they got a registered trademark on the color pink from the US Patent and Trademark Office. In the 1960s, Peter Sellers starred in a number of successful Pink Panther movies. Owens Corning took a license from the movie studio and has used the "spokestoon" to drive home that *pink* refers to their product. So the color idea came first; the movie license was an add-on. Notice that this license has continued for over 50 years and is likely to be perpetual.

Many have long forgotten ValuJet. It may be remembered by its more recent name, AirTran, which was later purchased by Southwest.

In 1996, ValuJet suffered a terrible plane crash in the Everglades. Its brand equity was pretty much zeroed out because the crash which was found to be related to mishandling of oxygen cylinders by airline staff. The company decided to reopen under a new brand name. So what does it cost to rebrand an airline? Marketing experts were queried on what it would cost to create enough (positive) brand awareness to start a small airline and get its planes full in a few months. The number was in the neighborhood of $20-50 million.

At the time, a well-known brand, PAN AM, was for sale for a mere $1.4 million. For reasons unknown, ValueJet didn't buy the brand, though it might have saved them at least $25 million. Had they made the PanAm brand purchase, perhaps AirTran (PanAm) would have been big enough to purchase Southwest. At least AirTran would have had saved a lot of marketing dollars to spend on new routes.

Some years ago, a marketer for Mayo Clinic told the story about how Mayo got into the brand licensing business. For all of Mayo's 100+ year history, until about 15 years ago, Mayo refused to license its brand to anyone. Hundreds of thousands of patients had passed through Mayo's clinics and hospitals over the years, many of them having been cured of serious illnesses. As a natural consequence, many wanted a memento of their stay. Unlike hotels, where the shampoo might carry the house brand, Mayo had nothing. And patients and visitors kept asking.

Market forces being what they are, Mayo started to find counterfeit products on the market. Obviously none of these were authorized by

Mayo. What finally drove them to relent on their refusal to license was the appearance of the (counterfeit) Mayo Clinic brand *Home Surgery Kit* complete with X-Acto® knife. Not only was it fake, but it was dangerous, and the Mayo name was on it! Knowing that they could never stop all of the counterfeits, it was time to make licenses available to those who would truly support the Mayo mission and brand. (Checking eBay for that Mayo home surgery kit, it appears that they are currently out of stock, but please, do check back later.)

Caveat to licensors: Be careful

Advice to licensees: licenses, under the right terms, are often a terrific deal.

Advice to licensors: licenses are always dangerous. Be aware of the risks.

Risks:

1. Licensees may damage your brand. Poorly made products, child labor law violations, dangerous additives in the product – these are potential hazards. Just read the newspapers.
2. The licensee may become so significant to the brand that it will change the brand's positioning. This may seem like an odd risk, but what if the Polaroid brand was licensed for sport shoes and was a big hit? It might change perception of the Polaroid brand forever.
3. The licensee could go bankrupt, and the bankruptcy court is relatively free to sell the license to someone who would make a doubtful licensee.

No matter how hard a licensor company tries, if it loses control of any aspect of production, it may get into deep trouble. That is what happened to McDonald's, KFC, Starbucks and others in China. Their brands in China have been severely damaged. In retrospect, they might not have licensed the brand at all.

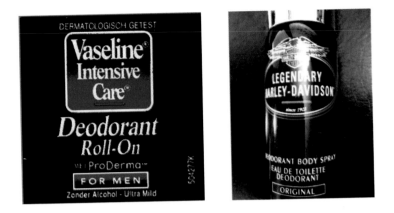

These two brands are familiar, but they are not known for this type of product. What is the viscosity of Vaseline roll-on? What is the smell of Harley deodorant? Neither of these products is sold in the US, but should the company have licensed them even in Europe? A brand either stands for **one** thing or it stands for **nothing**. Licensing revenue is a tasty morsel, but it is never worth risking damage to the core brand.

The ultimate danger to the licensor: licensee bankruptcy

Finally, you need to know this reality: the brand license of a bankrupt licensee does not revert to the licensor! It is an asset which the US Bankruptcy Court can use to generate revenue for the debtors of the bankrupt company. That means a licensor may well lose the right to choose who the next licensees are. There may be an opportunity to enforce quality control, but that doesn't always catch the bad guys in time. There is pretty much no way to prevent this, no matter how well drafted the license agreement is. Licensor beware!

It's been demonstrated that brand licenses are often a great deal for the licensee, but they can be risky for the licensor. You'd think that these tales of licensing horror would scare the licensors of successful brands from granting licenses. Not a chance.

As long as there is greed, there will be licensors. Greed is perhaps the second most powerful force, after water. Licensors make a lot of money, and the guy within the licensor company who grants the license is not usually the guy who has to clean up a licensing mess when things go wrong. Licensors are getting smarter. They have a legal obligation to enforce quality. Some are actually doing it. Smart licensors can minimize a lot of the risk; really smart licensors will make sure their brand positioning is not affected by the license, but there will still be some risk.

From a licensees' point of view, licensing is mostly a no-brainer. Some of the key questions to answer are:

1. Can the license be renewed, perhaps in perpetuity?
2. Under what circumstances can the license be cancelled?
3. Is there an annual minimum payment, regardless of sales?
4. Does the licensee have freedom to modify the mark in small ways?

Brand licensing is a very sophisticated field. Get good legal help with experience in this area, whether you are a licensor or licensee.

Bootstrapping your company's new brand through a *co-brand* license

The obvious downside to being a licensee is that you are not building *your* brand. That is the price of skipping the brand-building step. But what if you could bootstrap a brand license and build your brand too? Many licensors will not allow this bootstrapping because they know you will ultimately not need them once your brand is successful.

This is a tricky business, but it can be very effective. The examples above are famous brands using other famous brands, but a brand doesn't have to be famous to benefit from the bootstrap.

Takeaways for this chapter:

1. Licensing works great for licensees. It can be risky for licensors. The cost of a license is rarely more than the return on investment.

2. The hard part of licensing is getting a good brand. Look at Target's clever choice of Car and Driver as a guide.

3. Don't negotiate a license by yourself. Get a lawyer who knows the field.

Chapter 9

Tricky Brand Maneuvers

International and personal brands

Skip this chapter if:

1. Your company will *never* sell its products or services outside the USA,
2. You will never receive an international order (including Canada) from your website,
3. You won't mind if a Chinese company is using your brand to sell its products outside the US, or
4. You never use a personality (including yourself) to promote your brand.

For everyone else, it is critical that you anticipate your international expansion before you create your domestic (i.e., US) brand; trademark rules outside the US are very different, and your brand must conform to everyone's rules, not just the lowest common denominator's (that is, the US's). The cost of fixing an international mistake vs. avoiding one is roughly 10,000:1. That is, for every dollar spent proactively to avoid an international brand problem, fixing it will cost 1,000 to 10,000 times as much, if it can be fixed at all. That says something about the importance of spending some money to save a lot of money. Being financially proactive in this area is essential.

International Branding

In international branding there are two kinds of mistakes: linguistic (cultural) and legal. Both kinds will be discussed in this chapter. While the first kind is relatively easy to avoid, the second, legal, can be very tricky.

Linguistic and cultural mistakes

Linguistic and cultural mistakes are relatively easy to prevent, but prevention requires something few companies are willing to do: *before* even settling on a US (domestic) brand, making sure your brand reads well in foreign languages, including foreign slang.

Most of us have heard of the classic mistakes, like KFC's translation of *Finger Lickin' Good* into Chinese as "Bite your fingers off." There was Chevrolet Nova, where "nova" means "won't go" in Spanish, and Pepsi's "Pepsi adds life" campaign, which translated to Chinese is "We bring your ancestors back from the grave." These are more humorous than instructive. To get a better sense of how serious these mistakes are, note the following *foreign* mistakes from an English speaker's point of view:

These examples are from Sweden, a country where almost everyone speaks English. Kräpp, which literally means crepe paper, is clearly not coming to the US anytime soon, in single or double size packages.

This enticing product is from Finland, another country where English is widely spoken. It is windshield washer fluid and it is blue in color. The rest of the ingredients are anybody's guess, but if this is one of those descriptive brands, you know the ingredients. Notice that the words **Super** and **Blue** *are* in English, so one has to assume that the middle word is intended to have its English meaning as well. Not so good for the US market.

This is a bicycle bag made by a *US* company, Cannondale. The word under its logo is not used in polite company in the UK, where a naïve young college student (this book's author) purchased it, and toured the

UK by bicycle amusing and offending all Brits who got a good look. Cannondale has no recollection of this product.

This is a popular water product in Japan and a breakfast cereal in France.

The point is that it's easy to see how a domestic brand does not automatically qualify as a world brand for linguistic or cultural reasons. It's crucial to do the homework before an international launch.

The fix

The solution for linguistic mistakes like these is pretty obvious:

1. Assume that a North American brand will at least flow into a French (Quebec) and Spanish (Mexico or Spanish-speaking Americas) market even if it's not intended for export, so it must be acceptable in Spanish and French.
2. Assume that there is a likelihood of your product going international in the future. Plan for it now instead of hoping that the brand works overseas. Do a careful linguistic screen at the same time as the trademark clearance search.

3. At a minimum, run a Google® translation check of the proposed (or present!) brands through all languages.
4. Google translate will not pick up corrupted spellings and slang, so working with native speakers is the only safe way to go. There are services which can do this checking.
5. Remember that languages like Spanish are spoken in many countries and have different slang in each. You must check them all.

Legal mistakes

It is relatively easy to avoid the cultural and linguistic traps above. The legal traps are much more common, deadlier, and difficult to spot.

The most common legal mistake: Not registering the trademark (and domain) into countries the company may later expand or in countries where counterfeiters are common.

The typical expansion countries for US-based companies, depending on the products or services, are:

Canada

Mexico

EU

Australia

These countries are either geographically close to the US or have relatively low barriers to entry. On the other hand, the following is an abbreviated list of what might be considered to be challenging or **high risk**, or have **barriers**:

China/Hong Kong

Singapore

Taiwan

Malaysia

India

Korea

Japan

Indonesia

Brazil

These are high risk countries because they are either in locations where exports are very difficult due to various non-tariff barriers (Japan, India, Brazil), or have a well-proven propensity to pick and copy US brands. There are many more countries which could fit on this list.

Because these high risk countries are not likely to be first tier target markets for your brand, they are much more likely to be dismissed as unimportant. And, if your US brand name was registered by a trademark squatter in one of these countries before you got around to registering there, you would have to try to *buy it back*. It is a well-known form of ransom. To make matters worse, what if your brand was being used on inferior goods? Even assuming none of these inferior products will ever arrive on US shores, the brand damage will still be considerable. Imagine if Cartier had not registered its trademark in India and a company there made products of unknown quality bearing the name Cartier! To make matters worse, these inferior products were sold not only in India, but also in 150 other smaller countries, where neither company had registered the mark. Chances are, the Cartier name would suffer severe damage.

Keep in mind, registering someone else's trademark in a foreign country ("squatting") is NOT counterfeiting. It is perfectly legal for a "brand entrepreneur" to register your US brand in their country. Most countries do not have effective prohibitions against this, and as it is a great source of revenue, governments have no motivation to stop it.

Getting a brand back from a brand squatter is always costly, and often fails to recover the brand in the end. The brand squatter has little motivation to sell it back unless the numbers are really large, usually delusionally high.

Here are some rules to live by with respect to international branding:

Warning 1: It's the Wild West out there (in many foreign countries).

The moment you launch your brand, the race is on. Anyone with a computer can determine that you have launched your brand or filed your trademark application in the US Trademark Office. Once a US application is filed, by international treaty, the filer gets a six month head start on the brand squatters. Here's how it works. When one files a US trademark application, they are granted a six month grace period to file in other countries. If they file overseas within the grace period, the foreign trademark filing gets the same date as the US filing date. This can be important. If a trademark squatter monitors US trademark filings, he/she will not be able to beat your filing date in that country, *provided* you filed within the grace period. There is no extension on the six months. Use the time wisely. Plan your foreign trademark filing strategy. After the six months, it's open season on your brand, regardless of the country.

By the way, the same squatting system works for domains, but in the case of domains there is no six month grace period. Some guy in

Malaysia, China, or wherever, sees your registered US .com domain. He/she then registers that same domain name for $10 in his/her home country, and then just waits for your company to show up to buy the name back. Cybersquatting is also entirely legal and is a well-accepted practice everywhere, including in the US.

There is a trademark equivalent to domain cybersquatting. It works the same way but is far more damaging. A domain might not be needed, but a trademark is. For example, in Mexico, you cannot manufacture branded goods within the country using a trademark owned by another party, even if the goods are entirely for *export* out of Mexico. If goods are manufactured in Juarez, Mexico, for transfer to El Paso, Texas, and they contain a trademark owned by someone else in Mexico, the goods are potentially subject to seizure in Mexico. Consequently there is a thriving trade in Mexico and elsewhere to buy trademarks and sell them back for vast sums later, to US owners.

Suppose a product is selling well in the US. Now the company wants to export it to India, but someone else owns the trademark in India in that class of goods. There is a risk of having these products impounded at the dock. A nasty surprise on launch day in that country.

If that's not wild-west enough, here is the coup de grâce: in almost all countries except the US, it is possible to register a trademark for any goods/services *without having any intention to use the mark*. That means anyone with a few hundred dollars can scoop up a brand and hold it for at least three to five years for the mere purpose of blocking another's international expansion strategy. Even a competitor can buy the foreign trademark rights.

This is a common occurrence in China. A well-known American company discovered that its flagship brand was hijacked by a Chinese company (a competitor) who had no plans to use it but blocked expansion into China. For a few hundred dollars, they had command of the brand for the entire country of China simply because no one anticipated possible expansion there. The American company sued and won, but then the Chinese company appealed to the local People's court, conveniently located in the home town (in China) of the cybersquatter. This home town People's court had never heard a trademark or domain infringement case, but they sure did know who the "home team" was. The case is still pending. Stay tuned.

If a company has a website, advertises on the web, exhibits at US trade shows, or does anything other than hide in a cave, it is vulnerable to having its brand and domain hijacked overseas.

Warning 2: Being proactive is *much* cheaper than being reactive.

Remember Red Adair? He was the iconic king of oil well fire suppression. He capped all of the burning wells in Kuwait in nine months instead of the expected three to five years. He was expensive. As part of his fee, he demanded that the Kuwait government fly in an aircraft full of whiskey ("Do they want their fires out, or not?"). He got the whiskey. His fee was high, but he put out the fires years early. No matter what his fee was, it was less than the value of three years of burned oil.

The cost of filing trademark in foreign countries can get expensive. These fees are high, but in relation to what? The cost of doing something right has to be measured against the cost of fixing it later. The litigation to recover a trademark from a legitimate (non-counterfeit) owner, or to change brands in a foreign market, is easily 1,000-10,000x the cost of being proactive and securing international rights. Furthermore, in many cases litigation will fail. After all, trademark and domain squatting is not illegal, and then there is the matter of buying back the trademark for a *ransom price*, sometimes in the millions.

Some professional tricks to get out of a jam

There are lots of foreign risks. Here are some tricks to maximize what is most important:

1.   Conduct a trademark availability search in key foreign countries as you search in the US. Just because a trademark is available in the US does not mean that it isn't taken in other countries.

2. Don't squander your six month grace period. Decide which foreign markets are critical to you at the time of the US trademark filing. Six months goes fast.

Warning 3: Build a world brand from day one.

Weak (suggestive/descriptive) trademarks, which might work in the US, will almost always fail overseas.

The US legal framework is very lenient, allowing the registration (and ownership) of weak trademarks that are merely *capable* of developing acquired distinctiveness with enough advertising (recall The Weather Channel). The rest of the world has little tolerance for weak brands. Their dividing line is somewhere between suggestive and descriptive. Some countries are willing to push that line toward the US standard, while others, like the EU, are very strict. Since there are roughly 175 separate trademark jurisdictions worldwide with varying standards (and all are stricter than the US), your trademark should be strong enough to qualify for registration in the strictest country.

Consider the folks who invented the concept of parking a car off site from the airport and providing a shuttle to the airport departure door. Clever, but utterly unpatentable. That leaves trademark as the first and only line of defense against competition.

Since parking away from the airport and then flying was a new concept, potential customers were not going to know what this service was without some explanation. So, why not incorporate the *description* of what it is right into the brand? PARK your car AND then you FLY away.

In the US, Park 'N Fly was able to obtain limited trademark rights on a descriptive mark by massive marketing and recognition. They were clearly not able to stop others from using similar names.

As weak as their trademark rights are in the US, in most other countries, which do not recognize descriptive trademarks at all, Park 'N Fly would not be registerable, and consequently would have no defensible position against competitors. Perhaps Park 'N Fly never expects to operate overseas.

If, however, Park 'N Fly had chosen a mark that was distinctive, and well to the left of that dividing line (between suggestive and descriptive), the brand would be international-ready.

Not everyone followed Park 'N Fly's lead. Above are two examples of very strong trademarks in the same parking field.

The Hazards of Personal Brands

Whirlpool

The Maytag man, Gordon Jump, died in 2003. They replaced him with someone who sort of looked like him, but the Maytag man promotion withered away. Maytag forgot about mortality when they booked Gordon to be their lovable spokesperson.

Flo (Stephanie Courtney), the star of almost all Progressive Insurance commercials, is much younger, but since the 13th Amendment to the US Constitution, is free to quit working for Progressive anytime, no matter what her contracts says. We are told that she has made enough money on these commercials that she will never have to work again. That presents Progressive with a scary prospect.

Another personal brand hazard is overlooking the fact that people aren't always reliable.

On the other hand, animals (especially caricatures), inanimate objects, and symbols are typically a great deal more predictable. Hello Kitty

196

will never be found hobnobbing with the wrong kind of feline. The branding lesson is: Beware of using people as brands unless they are long dead and you have the rights to use their image.

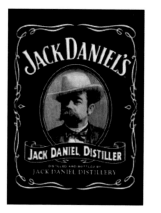 

Takeaways for this chapter:

1. International branding is very different from US domestic branding and very difficult, but it's manageable if you know the rules and pitfalls.
2. First come, first serve is the basic rule in foreign countries – register first or you will lose.
3. Cyber trademark squatters live off others' success. Don't think they aren't watching your brand.
4. Personal brands can be risky – consider caricature, animals, or dead people (where permitted by law).
5. In international matters, being proactive is much cheaper than being reactive.

Chapter 10

Ready to Launch

Summary

This chapter is intended to summarize the key points of each chapter, making it easier to refer back to them. While there is much more to know about building a valuable brand-centric company, if you integrate the contents of this book with your company's branding (or rebranding) process, you will be ahead of 99% of the other companies.

Chapter 1: Why building a brand-centric company is worth it. The difference between a brand-centric company and a company with a brand.

The purpose of Chapter 1 is to motivate you to *start* the process of building a valuable company. What makes companies *profitable* is not the same as what makes them *valuable*. Valuable companies are the sum of their assets, which, these days, are mostly intellectual property assets. Brands (trademarks) are worth phenomenal amounts of money – but only if you've taken the time to hone the brand's story (positioning) so it matters to the customer. Then the brand is really the storehouse of the company's reputation and wealth. If the brand is merely a name (yours) on the door, then the brand is a hollow one. When exiting your company sometime in the future, the difference between a huge payout and getting out for residual value will lie in what you did during the three to ten years prior to sale. If you are a public company, the stock price will be a reflection of the brand reputation. Just ask Apple Inc.

Chapter 1 gives many examples of the financial benefits of being a brand-based company, but if you are somehow unconvinced, there is another, critically important reason for starting: brand-based companies are better able to survive *disruptive change*. Disruptive change is change you don't see coming, and even if you do, you might not be able to get out of its way. Brand-based companies get through disruptive change much better. Ask Dolby Labs.

Your starting point is this mantra:

From now on, **each business decision must have a brand-building component** *or I will rethink that decision.*

Chapter 2: The curse of the ME company.

Since 98% of North American businesses are privately held, this chapter may well apply to you. You have built an amazing company, profitable, stable, a pillar of the community. But in all likelihood it isn't saleable because **you** are the company, and when you leave, so does the company's value. The key concept of this chapter is *transferable value*, which involves viewing your company's sale from the buyer's point of view. What they are looking to buy and what you *think* they want to buy often don't match, and it is only what *they* want that counts. In a word, they only want assets which can be transferred to them.

ME companies are IP-asset poor. If the real brand is the reputation of the founder, know that he/she is not for sale. Reputation must be converted into a *transferable asset* by infusing the reputation of the founder into the brand, not a person. It is a subtle but dramatic difference.

Unless you are that rare genius who figured this branding stuff out the day you started your business, more than likely you will need to make it your *mission* to become brand-centric. Otherwise it won't happen.

You also need to appoint a Brand Czar (CBO), which often is yourself as CEO.

The time to start is NOW. The operative word is: *start.*

Insisting that the brand concepts in this book don't apply to you, despite the myriad examples of how they do, is a surefire way to end up selling your company for salvage value.

One of the most important traits of a leader is to *know what you don't know.* This might be one of those times. The great news is that if you aren't a ME company, then this brand building process will only make you stronger and more valuable.

Chapter 3: Brand positioning.

This is critically important: in building a brand-centric company, you do *not* start with the brand. You start with the reason why customers love doing business with you. You have to reach deep into their mind and find the connection that matters. Then you have to stay true to that course, until you can't stand it anymore – and then *continue to stay the course.* Continuity wins every time.

The words that connect you to your customer are **rarely faster, better, cheaper**, even if you are indeed one or more of those. Those companies don't last.

An effective technique for finding your connection, your positioning, is to create the *perfect tag line* and work backwards to create the positioning statement.

Take the *elevator speech* test and see if yours is good enough to form the perfect tag line. You may find out that it needs a lot of reworking. That's fine. You will only make it better.

Without the foundation of this positioning, it is pretty near impossible to have an effective brand strategy. Your brand will be twisting in the wind, and your company will be defined by how your *competition* wants to portray your brand. That's never a good idea.

Chapter 3 is extremely important, so please don't skip it.

Chapter 4: The first rule of brands.

This chapter is about the first rule of trademarks: If *no one* can own your brand, then it is not actually a brand at all. You may have thought it was a brand, but it isn't. It's a generic or descriptive word, and you will never own it.

There is nothing more important about your brand than *whether you can own it.*

It's no different than owning your house or your car. If you are paying the mortgage on a house, and you didn't have clear title, you are throwing away your money. Continuing to pay will not get you clear title in cars, houses, or brands.

In the world of real estate and cars, there are systems in place that let you check the title to find out who owns it. Not so much with brands. More often than not, the party that *will* do an ownership check of your brand is your potential buyer. It's called *due diligence*, and it is not the time to find out you have a broken brand. Therefore, the time to determine ownership is NOW.

Identify whether you have a broken brand and fix it now. You can't make up lost time, but you *can* stop the brand equity hemorrhage.

Chapter 5: The second rule of brands.

The second rule of branding is also about ownership, but it's different than the first rule. It says: If *you* don't own your brand, and someone else does, you have no brand. You are wasting valuable time and money and accomplishing nothing. And unlike the scenario of Rule 1, you risk getting sued for trademark infringement.

Again, denial is not your friend. If you haven't been sued for years, you figure it won't ever happen. As an IP lawyer, I know that this is not so. This secret fault line in your company is going to appear someday and erase all the hard work you have put into building the brand – that you don't own. As before, judgment day is often during due diligence, when you try to sell your company or your division, or when you just bought 30 seconds of air time during the Super Bowl to promote your brand. The trademark zombies (common law trademark owners) will find you.

Like Rule 1, it is very risky to ignore Rule 2.

Chapter 6: A rescue plan.

There is a very good chance you may have discovered that some aspect of your brand violates Rule 1 or 2, or both. Or you have a ME company and never realized it. Even more likely, you will not be able to identify your brand position, or it no longer fits your company.

It makes sense to admit these weaknesses. Sometimes that means starting over. If that is the case, it is quite likely that you have such a problematic brand, that you have little brand equity to lose.

If your brand violates Rule 1 (it's not a brand), one option is to *add a brand* to your (non)brand. In the Chapter 6 example, we added *Wild Country* as a prefix to the descriptive brand Outdoor Towels. Will your customers notice? Sure. Will they desert you? Hardly. And you will start to build a brand-centric company from then on.

You may also need to file for federal trademark registration on the Supplemental trademark register. Get experienced legal help for this one.

Chapter 7: Power tools for serious brand-centric companies.

In addition to words, graphics (logos), color, tag lines, and shapes are also powerful elements of a *unified* brand strategy.

A unified brand strategy engages all of these elements in such a way that they reinforce each other.

The Rules of branding apply to these other types of brands in slightly nuanced ways. For example, color can be a part of the brand, but certain "functional" colors are inherently excluded. What makes a color functional will depend on your product or service. Colors needed for safety, like yellow and red, are the most common functional colors.

Shapes (both product and packaging) are powerful brands in themselves and can be protected by trademark law and *design* patent law. Design patents are easy to get and provide scary damages against infringers, but they must be applied very early in the design process or the time to file will expire. There are no time extensions for design patents.

Consistency is the hallmark of color/shape/graphic brands. The desire to "freshen up" a graphic image or change a color because of boredom is can be dangerous to accumulated brand equity. It is critically important that your company has a Brand Czar who understands this and has the power to enforce consistency and The Rules.

Chapter 8: The secret world of brand licensing.

Brand licensing is simply renting someone else's brand equity to get a jump start in the market. Like all renting, it's cheaper and faster than building your own, but you never own it. Considering that it is possible to rent forever, sometimes it is just as good as creating your own. The prime reason to take a brand license is that you immediately benefit from the great branding of other companies. It is far faster and has a greater probability of success than going it alone. When you sell the company, you won't get the giant return you would get if you had built its brand yourself, but you also won't have taken nearly as much risk or spent as much.

The keys to success are: 1) get the right brand, which is rarely the brand leader in the category, but a tangentially related brand (see the "Car the Driver" brand story in this chapter), and 2) negotiate a good license agreement. There are no "standard" terms. Everything is negotiable. Unless you are a brand licensing lawyer, you can't do this yourself or you will be eaten alive. Get experienced legal help.

Chapter 9: Tricky brand issues – international and personal brands.

This chapter is about two especially sophisticated yet thorny problems in branding: international branding and the use of living people as brands.

International branding is complicated for many reasons, but the single most important piece of advice you need is: plan in advance for your international expansion. If you don't, there is a very good chance your brands will be taken by others by the time you expand to other countries.

Foreign trademark laws are different, most importantly, in that they generally don't recognize descriptive and weak *suggestive* trademarks. So, if you want to have a shot at foreign protection, you need to select a strong US brand first.

Also, just as US brands need a clearance/availability search, careful searches are needed in foreign countries as well. There is no logical reason to assume that a brand is available in a foreign country just because it is available in the US.

There is an automatic six month grace period to file in foreign countries beginning at the time the US trademark application is filed. This time goes fast, so you very much need to plan at the time of the US filing. When your grace period expires, anyone in another country can file for your trademark, effectively blocking your expansion in that country.

Often, by accident or intention, a person becomes a company's brand. Neither is a good idea. Founders like to be brands, but that insures their companies are ME companies, and hence their brand has little transferable value. Making a *person* a part of a brand is almost always a bad idea. People do things that the company might not approve of, including transgressing the company's values, quitting, or dying. When they do, they take the company's brand equity with them. Consider cartoons or animals. Who can resist a spokes-kitten?

Chapter 10

Well, that's this chapter, so this is the last opportunity to give two final pieces of advice that will make all the difference in building a brand-centric company:

1. **Start.** Scientific evidence proves that failing to *start* the process of building a brand-centric company will result in never building one. Even if you start slowly, brand building is like drops of water on a stone. Eventually it will produce results and make your company stronger, more profitable and valuable, and thus more saleable.

2. **Don't Quit.** Don't expect to notice immediate results. You are in the brand forest and can't see the big picture. Remember the mantra: consider every business decision from the perspective of how it will benefit the brand. Make sure your employees do the same. Once you get traction, it will be like a moving train – hard to stop. Don't let others tell you it isn't working. It is. You just can't measure it for a long time.

You can really get there.

www.brandcentering.com

Acknowledgement: Zombie image used under the Creative Commons license, unmodified http://www.vectorfree.com/zombies-silhouettes-pack